SHARED STRATEGIES FOR THE CAREER ADVANCEMENTS OF ASSISTANT PRINCIPALS

DISSERTATION MADE INTO A BOOK

BY

DR. TIFFANY MCMILLIAN BURKS

DEDICATION

Thankful to Jesus Christ who gave me the wisdom and strength to transform my dissertation into a book that in hopes will allow universities, districts, and schools to take a closer look with intentionality in preparing future leaders.

Those of you who are in a educational leadership role this book is dedicated to you. I know how hard it is to work with the right heart to serve students and the community and still get passed by because of the politics in such a stressful position.

This book is to encourage you to not give up on your dreams to improve schools and make school a base for continuos learning.

ACKNOWLEDGMENT

In the journey through this dissertation, I encountered challenges that ultimately revealed the profound significance of support and care. The encouragement I received proved to be a driving force that propelled me to complete this endeavor, reinforcing the belief that my voice holds vital power and that I can effect positive change in the lives of others. My vision to ensure equitable leadership mentorship for all and the establishment of standards aligned with leadership growth emerged as a guiding light.

With seven years of experience as an Assistant Principal, I witnessed the unfortunate reality of highly qualified individuals being overlooked for principalship positions due to the prevailing "good old boy system" and the adage "it's not what you know, but who you know." My exposure to these biases further solidified my commitment to advocate for mentorship and proper coaching as a professional courtesy, fostering a culture where principals mentor Assistant Principals based on evaluation goals rather than personal biases.

This journey of revelation and transformation led me to comprehend how biases constrict opportunities. Amidst these challenges, I found solace in the unwavering support provided by people orchestrated by God. I am forever grateful for the divine interventions that have paved my path to this point of triumph.

Throughout this process, the divine presence of Elohim has been undeniable. Miracles unfurled in the form of childcare, self-care, and daycare, underscoring the incredible power of faith. I extend my heartfelt gratitude to my dissertation chair, Dr. Linda Wilson-Jones, whose unwavering support instilled in me the confidence to persevere. Dr. Landon Hadley's exemplary role modeling and Dr. Paris Jones' honesty and care have been instrumental. Dr. Ashley Johnson whose expertise and knowledge was the foundation to move forward.

To the esteemed faculty and staff of Fayetteville State University Leadership Program, I am indebted for the exceptional education and the opportunity to ascend to new heights of academic success.

In the chorus of gratitude, I honor my little cousin Victoria, her childlike faith and innocent inquiry fueled my educational journey. My mother, Hermine Dunk, stood as an unwavering pillar of belief, constantly affirming that "God's got You."

To my children – Devin, Harmony, Justice, Mariah, and Jeremiah – your unwavering support has been the driving force beneath my wings.

James Earl Dunk, my stepdad, raised me with compassion and conviction, leaving an indelible mark on my journey. To my late father, David Smith, your absence is deeply felt, yet I know you would be proud.

Monica Williams-Jackson, my best friend from middle school and college roommate, though taken too soon, left an enduring legacy of dedication to education.

My extended family – the Thompsons, Richardsons, McMillians, Bakers, Dunks, and Smiths – have provided impeccable support. My friends, church family, and co-workers have become my foundation. Our collective faith has moved mountains and for that, I am immeasurably grateful.

TABLE OF CONTENTS

CHAPTER 1
INTRODUCTION

In the realm of educational leadership, the journey from Assistant Principal to Principal is a transformative odyssey that shapes not only individuals but also the institutions they guide. This chapter unravels the intricate tapestry of preparing Assistant Principals who aspire to ascend the echelons of educational leadership, paving their way to becoming effective Principals.

SETTING THE STAGE: PREPARING FOR PRINCIPALSHIP

At the heart of this exploration lies the preparatory process that weaves together the mentorship, guidance, and development essential for Assistant Principals on their path to Principalship. The study undertaken dives into the standards and evaluative tools that anchor these obligations, acting as guiding beacons through the developmental journey.

EQUITY AND OPPORTUNITY: THE ROLE OF DISTRICTS

Within the fabric of educational progress, districts bear the responsibility of ensuring uniformity and equity. This chapter advocates the vital need for accountability measures within districts to ensure that every Assistant Principal receives equal and ample opportunities for growth and mentorship under the stewardship of seasoned Principals.

THE PIPELINE DILEMMA: FROM EXCLUSION TO EMPOWERMENT

Assistant Principals are often regarded as the future torchbearers of school leadership, poised to ascend to Principal roles. Yet, their potential is too often hindered by the shadow of exclusion from significant leadership prospects. This chapter casts light upon the challenge of nurturing these candidates and illuminates their journey toward empowerment.

FORGING THE PRINCIPAL'S CRUCIBLE: EDUCATION AND INTERNSHIPS

The Assistant Principals of today are shaped through comprehensive educational programs, often undergoing internships that prime them for their roles. This chapter delves into the foundations laid during these formative periods and how they contributed to the evolution of Assistant Principals.

LEADERSHIP ALCHEMY: THE PRINCIPAL'S ROLE IN MENTORING

At the heart of effective mentorship lies the Principal's leadership style, roles, perceptions, and expectations. These elements form the crucible within which Assistant Principals are forged into adept leaders, with the guidance and insights they need to excel in their journey toward Principalship.

EXPANDING HORIZONS: THE EVOLUTION OF ASSISTANT PRINCIPALS' ROLES

Meeting the rigorous standards of educational reform requires Assistant Principals to transcend the realm of mere discipline and attendance. This chapter advocates for the metamorphosis of their roles into equity-conscious instructional leaders, carrying the torch of change toward a more inclusive and progressive educational landscape.

DISTINGUISHED BY LEADERSHIP: PIONEERS VS. MANAGERS

Drawing on the wisdom of scholars, this chapter distinguishes between leadership and management, painting a portrait of the visionary Principal who inspires others to achieve collective goals, in contrast to the managerial role of overseeing specific tasks.

EDUCATION'S NORTH STAR: VISION, STRATEGY, AND STUDENT ACHIEVEMENT

The educational journey is guided by a district's vision, strategy, and mission. This chapter underscores the central importance of these elements, emphasizing that the ultimate driving force is the achievement and success of students, breathing life into educational organizations.

NAVIGATING COMPLEXITY: CHALLENGES AND PRINCIPAL'S TIME

In the ever-changing landscape of education, the mantle of school leadership has grown increasingly complex. Mandated reforms, shifting demographics, technological advancements, financial constraints, and evolving expectations have reshaped the terrain. This chapter elucidates

the evolving nature of these challenges, exploring
how they impact the time available for Principals to
mentor and coach Assistant Principals.

SCULPTING SCHOOL HIERARCHIES: THE ROLE OF ASSISTANT PRINCIPALS

As integral members of the school
organization, Assistant Principals stand as the
linchpin, enabling the seamless continuation of the
school's operations in the Principal's absence. This
chapter unveils the multifaceted role they play
within the intricate tapestry of the school
community.

FROM APPRENTICE TO MAESTRO: PREPARING FOR THE PRINCIPALSHIP

As the stage for transformation is set, this
chapter underscores the significance of Assistant
Principals comprehending the requirements of
Principalship. Completion of preparation programs
that equip them for this demanding role is
advocated, echoing the wisdom of scholars and
researchers.

THE PATH UNPAVED: BRIDGING THE TRAINING GAP

Recent research has exposed a gap in the preparation of Assistant Principals for the eventual transition into Principal roles. This chapter amplifies the need to bridge this training gap, ensuring that aspiring Principals are adequately prepared to shoulder the multifaceted responsibilities that await them.

BEYOND NUMBERS: ASSISTANT PRINCIPALS AS SCHOOL LEADERS

Assistant Principals form a significant majority among school administrators, their responsibilities and duties as diverse as the schools they serve. This chapter magnifies the nuanced nature of their roles, acknowledging that their contributions are pivotal to the school's success.

EMPOWERING LEADERSHIP: LEGAL AND ADMINISTRATIVE DIMENSIONS

Drawing from the legal compass of the Individuals with Disabilities Act, this chapter establishes the framework of administrative responsibilities and instructional leadership that Principals are entrusted with. Under the watchful gaze of the superintendent, their roles guide the planning, operation, and evaluation of educational programs.

In this inaugural chapter, we embark on a journey that traverses the rich landscape of educational leadership, from the aspirations of Assistant Principals to the intricate threads of mentorship, legal obligations, and the ever-evolving role of school leaders. As we delve deeper into the following chapters, the narrative will continue to unfold, painting a comprehensive portrait of how Assistant Principals can transform into Principals of influence, vision, and impact.

CHAPTER 2: NURTURING LEADERSHIP
FROM MENTORSHIP TO TRANSFORMATION

In this chapter, we delve deep into the intricate landscape of educational leadership, focusing on the principal's multifaceted role as both the instructional leader and mentor to their assistant principal. The journey of shared leadership and the transformative power of mentorship will be illuminated. This chapter unfolds across several thematic domains, each offering profound insights into the world of educational leadership:

MENTORING AND LEADERSHIP ADVANCEMENT

Mentoring is an age-old practice that has left an indelible mark on the growth and development of individuals, be it in the workplace, academia, or the lives of youth. Chickering (1969) emphasized the significance of student-faculty interactions in shaping student identity and fostering academic success. Moreover, mentoring has shown to bolster resilience and reduce conduct disorders in at-risk youth (Masten & Garmezy, 1985; Rutter, 1987). The benefits of mentorship extend to psychological well-being, academic achievements, and positive perceptions, impacting both mentees and mentors alike (Lockwood et al., 2010). Such bonds are symbiotic, nurturing personal fulfillment and job performance in mentors (Bass, 1990; Newby & Corner, 1997; Ramaswami & Dreher, 2007).

Recent studies reveal a profound connection between job satisfaction and student achievement among teachers and principals (Dicke et al., 2020). High levels of job satisfaction emerge in environments where student achievement flourishes. Principals play a pivotal role in fostering this environment, creating a positive climate, and serving as mentors to their assistant principals. The intersection of transformational leadership, which we will explore further, plays a pivotal role in this process.

LEADERSHIP HISTORICAL BACKGROUND OF LEADERSHIP DEVELOPMENT

The exploration of leadership's historical evolution takes us back to Galton's Great Man theory, which laid the foundation for understanding leadership (Clark & Clark, 1990). Leadership, however, transcends time and gender boundaries, consistently proving to be a cornerstone of effective organizational and societal functioning (Day & Johansson, 2008). Leadership has been a subject of rigorous study in the realm of social science (Day & Johansson, 2008), birthing myriad theories, each reflecting the dynamic nature of leadership (Fiedler, 1971).

Leadership isn't confined to a singular sphere; it encompasses various levels of engagement. At the supervisory level, leaders complement organizational systems, set group goals, and integrate diverse individual styles. They maximize the collective abilities of their team and facilitate conflict resolution (Katz & Kahn, 1978). Strategically, leadership ensures the organization's coordinated functionality amidst a dynamic external environment, intertwining with the core tenets of transformational leadership, which we'll soon explore.

SELF-EFFICACY AND LEADERSHIP

This study delves into the effectiveness of strategies implemented by principals to prepare their assistant principals for the pivotal transition to principalship. It is an evolution driven by the unique needs of diverse communities. Principal supervisors emerge as crucial agents of support and

development in this process (Goldring et al., 2018).
When principals mentor and lead with care,
assistant principals are better equipped to assume
leadership in their absence.

Self-efficacy, akin to the wind beneath one's
wings, plays a pivotal role in this developmental
journey. It is the perception of one's capability to
influence change, a hidden motivator steering the
principal's actions (Özdemir, 2018). Through
performance accomplishments, modeling, and
verbal persuasion, principals can instill self-efficacy
beliefs in their assistant principals (Bandura, 1997).
This process can make or break an assistant
principal's spirit, determining their readiness to take
the helm as a principal.

TRANSFORMATIONAL LEADERSHIP

Transformational leadership emerges as a
beacon guiding this transformative journey. Rooted
in the ancient echoes of time, the concept of
mentoring traces back to Homer's Odyssey, where
Odysseus entrusted his mentor to guide his son.
Scholarly exploration into mentoring started with
Levinson's seminal work, "The Seasons of a Man's
Life" (Levinson et al., 1978), emphasizing the
pivotal role of mentoring relationships in human

development. It highlighted that the absence of an effective mentor was akin to poor parenting in childhood (Lee et al., 2020).

As the educational landscape evolved, so did leadership theories. From Galton's Great Man theory, we traverse through the annals of leadership history, witnessing the ever-expanding role of leaders irrespective of gender (Day & Johansson, 2008). Leadership scholars have meticulously dissected this complex phenomenon, birthing a multitude of theories (Bennis, 2007).

Transformational leadership, a cornerstone of modern leadership theories, has demonstrated its prowess in shaping work-related attitudes and behaviors, such as job satisfaction (Bass et al., 2003; Kovjanic et al., 2013). Principals are the custodians of vision, mission, and goals, ensuring their alignment with the aspirations of the school community.

LEADERS SETTING THE EXAMPLE

The journey of leadership is not always paved with roses. Some principals, driven by personal agendas or nepotistic networks, may falter in their leadership roles. This can lead to ineffective mentorship, hindering the development of assistant

principals. Such leaders may create hostile
environments, stifling growth.

In contrast, a principled and ethical leader
understands the weight of their role. Accountability
becomes paramount, and trust is fostered,
encompassing trust in the person, trust in the
profession, and trust in the process (Smith &
Benavot, 2019). The principal must be the living
embodiment of the expectations, demonstrating
integrity, and modeling the desired behavior. This
transformative leadership, built on positive
relationships and sincerity, catalyzes change within
the organization.

However, not all leadership journeys are
virtuous. In academia, instances of bullying and
toxic leadership can surface, casting shadows on
educational institutions (Frazier, 2011). Principals
must align their moral compass and fulfill their
professional obligation to their assistant principals,
students, and staff. Toxic leadership breeds toxic
environments, but principled leadership fosters
positivity and progress.

This chapter peels back the layers of
educational leadership, revealing the pivotal role of
mentorship and transformational leadership in
shaping leaders of tomorrow. It underscores the

13

necessity for principled and ethical leadership, for in the hands of these leaders, the future of education thrives or withers.

RETHINKING THE EDUCATIONAL FRAMEWORK DURING COVID-19

The COVID-19 pandemic, which emerged in early 2020, presented the education sector with an unprecedented and formidable challenge. The rapid spread of the virus compelled governments worldwide to take drastic measures, including the temporary closure of educational institutions to contain the contagion (Zhu & Liu, 2020). These measures led to an abrupt and seismic shift in how education was delivered, impacting educators and leaders at all levels. This chapter explores the profound transformation of education during the pandemic, the evolving roles and responsibilities of educational leaders, and the multifaceted challenges faced by schools during this critical period.

THE ADVENT OF REMOTE LEARNING

The transition from traditional face-to-face learning to remote education represented a fundamental paradigm shift in the field of education. Online learning, defined as educational experiences that occur either synchronously or asynchronously through various technology tools with internet access (Smalley et al., 2021), emerged as the cornerstone of this transformation. It required a complete reimagining of the educational process, redefining not only how students and teachers interacted but also the roles of school leaders.

The move to remote learning was not without its challenges. Educators and leaders found themselves navigating uncharted territory, grappling with technology, and adapting to new pedagogical approaches (Jandrić et al., 2018). The pandemic necessitated conceptual and philosophical rethinking of teaching and learning, the relationship dynamics between educators and students, and the incorporation of technology within post-digital learning communities (Jandrić et al., 2018).

LEADERSHIP AMIDST CRISIS

Amidst the turmoil of the COVID-19 pandemic, educational leaders, particularly principals, found themselves thrust into a new reality. Their roles transcended traditional boundaries, encompassing responsibilities that extended far beyond the conventional scope of their positions (Smalley et al., 2021). These leaders faced the arduous task of maintaining their leadership

15

roles while fulfilling their obligations in the face of a crisis that brought unprecedented logistical complexities (Gordon & Reber, 2020).

One of the foremost challenges was the rapid shift to remote learning, which had a profound impact on educational leadership. The pandemic's financial implications, coupled with the necessity for innovative solutions, prompted a reevaluation of the traditional educational framework (Zhu & Liu, 2020). In this evolving landscape, principals played a pivotal role in forging partnerships and creating collaborative strategies among school board members, district leaders, teachers, and teacher assistants.

VIRTUAL MENTORSHIP AND LEADERSHIP DEVELOPMENT

The pandemic disrupted the usual avenues of interaction and mentorship that assistant principals typically experience in a face-to-face setting. However, it also accelerated the adoption of virtual platforms for mentorship and leadership development (Smalley et al., 2021). Educational leaders turned to technology to continue guiding and supporting assistant principals, ensuring that they received the mentorship required for their growth, even in virtual spaces.

The COVID-19 crisis forced educational leaders to question and re-envision the traditional educational framework. Some school districts transitioned entirely to virtual learning, while others adopted hybrid approaches, combining in-person and remote instruction (Zhu & Liu, 2020). This crisis became an opportunity for educators to transcend the confines of physical classrooms and unite in their commitment to reach all students and provide equitable education.

CHALLENGES AND DECISIONS

The pandemic's impact extended beyond classrooms and leadership roles, deeply affecting the mental and emotional well-being of educators, students, and families. The uncertainty of the situation weighed heavily on educators, including principals and teachers, who had to make life-altering decisions regarding their work environments (Zhu & Liu, 2020).

The boundary between returning to in-person teaching, potentially jeopardizing their health, and resigning from their positions became increasingly blurred. The pandemic's stress, stemming from the

17

uncertainty surrounding classroom settings, prompted some educators to resign (Sahu, 2020). Moreover, the mental health of students who lacked access to remote learning facilities emerged as a critical concern.

RESILIENCE AND ADAPTABILITY IN EDUCATIONAL LEADERSHIP

In summary, this chapter has provided an in-depth exploration of the profound transformation of education during the COVID-19 pandemic. The shift to remote learning challenged educators and leaders alike, prompting a reevaluation of the traditional educational framework. Principals emerged as resilient and adaptable leaders, steering their schools through uncharted waters.

The pandemic underscored the need for flexible and dynamic leadership in education. As the education sector moves forward, the lessons learned during this crisis must be carried forward, shaping a more resilient and adaptable future for generations to come. This chapter has offered a comprehensive analysis of the multifaceted challenges and opportunities that emerged during this critical period in the world of education.

POLITICS IN EDUCATION

The realm of education exists at the intersection of politics and societal demands. Invariably, politics and market forces permeate the educational landscape, and the challenge lies in harmonizing them with community needs and public expectations, forging a mutually beneficial relationship for all stakeholders (Baig et al., 2022). It's imperative to recognize that the power of politics can be harnessed for positive outcomes, rather than viewing it through a negative lens (Baig et al., 2022). This chapter delves into the intricate dynamics of politics within education, the journey of assistant principals aiming for principal roles, and the critical concept of accountability in educational leadership.

HARNESSING THE POWER OF POLITICS IN EDUCATION

Education, often deemed the cornerstone of societal progress, holds a prominent place in the functions of state and local governments (Brown v. Board of Education, 2022). The role of politics in shaping educational policy, funding, and priorities is undeniable. Yet, the key lies in utilizing political forces constructively, aligning them with community needs and public expectations. This

19

approach strives for a harmonious coexistence where education becomes a driving force for societal betterment.

In a world marked by complex challenges, educational leaders are instrumental in navigating the intricate intersection of politics and education. Their role extends beyond the confines of educational institutions. It encompasses advocating for policies that foster equitable access to quality education, addressing the concerns of diverse stakeholders, and promoting educational reforms that align with societal needs. Principals and assistant principals shoulder the responsibility of ensuring that politics in education serves as a force for positive change.

THE REALITIES OF ASSISTANT PRINCIPALS SEEKING PRINCIPAL ROLES

Assistant principals, driven by ambition and dedication, often set their sights on becoming principals. This aspiration, however, unveils a series of harsh realities. To bridge the gap between the roles, assistant principals must embrace mentorship, a transformative journey that reveals the true nature of leadership beyond the allure of financial promotions. As Sun (2018) notes, some assistant principals opt to remain in their current roles, eschewing the path to principalship, recognizing that each advancement brings a substantial escalation in responsibilities.

The principalship is multifaceted, requiring not only administrative skills but also the capacity to act as an instructional leader (Fullan, 2003; Halverson & Plecki, 2015; Sergiovanni, 2001). While assistant principals strive to ascend the educational hierarchy, they must continue to fulfill their roles as instructional leaders. The assistant principalship serves as an invaluable training ground, cultivating leadership skills that are essential in the principal's realm.

ACCOUNTABILITY MEASURES IN LEADERSHIP

Accountability is a cornerstone of the educational landscape, ensuring that individuals and organizations remain answerable for their actions within the educational system (National Open University of Nigeria, 2008). Absence of accountability often leads to uncertainty, irregularities, and injustice (Kalman & Gediklioğlu, 2014). In the realm of education, accountability is not merely a buzzword but a vital principle designed to protect all stakeholders, with a special focus on students.

Bovens (2007) defines accountability as a relationship between an actor (accountor) and a forum (accounted), where the actor bears the obligation to explain and justify their actions, while the forum can pose questions, pass judgments, and impose consequences. Educational administrators shoulder accountability not only to stakeholders but also for the accomplishment of educational goals, utilizing available resources and adopting globally accepted best practices in school administration.

In mentoring relationships, role accountability is paramount. Those undertaking leadership roles must be held accountable, transparently communicating performance expectations to stakeholders while providing justifications for accountability (Romzek et al., 2014). The principalship, with its hierarchical structure and clearly defined roles, embodies the essence of accountability. Principals navigate this landscape, continuously performing their duties as systems and potential actors, all while being observed and evaluated by various stakeholders (Frink & Klimoski, 2004).

SHARED RESPONSIBILITY FOR ACCOUNTABILITY

The conversation surrounding accountability in education has evolved over the years, particularly since the enactment of the No Child Left Behind Act (NCLB). Smith (Smith & Benavot, 2019) redirects this discourse toward a focus on how citizens can collaboratively share the responsibility for school success, in line with shared democratic goals. Within the educational hierarchy, a chain of command exists, reinforcing accountability mechanisms to ensure organizational needs are met. Principals, as accountable leaders, must operate with integrity, pursuing the needs of all stakeholders and contributing unselfishly to organizational improvement.

The value system of individuals in leadership positions significantly influences their decisions and actions. An individual's value system is a stable framework of beliefs and rules that guides decision-making, conflict resolution, and alternative selection (Sahin, 2004). Accountability, therefore, extends beyond policies and regulations; it encompasses the intrinsic values and ethical principles upheld by educational leaders.

ACCOUNTABILITY MEASURES IN EDUCATIONAL LEADERSHIP

In the realm of educational leadership, accountability is operationalized through professional learning plans. These plans provide a structured timeline and goal-oriented framework for individual growth and career development. While specific accountability measures may vary across districts, they typically involve periodic evaluations and documentation of professional development activities. Principals and assistant principals, as leaders, are responsible for charting their growth journeys, substantiating their progress with tangible artifacts, and fostering mentorship relationships throughout the process.

CHALLENGES IN EDUCATIONAL LEADERSHIP MENTORING

Mentorship plays a pivotal role in preparing future educational leaders. However, several challenges surround the mentoring process, particularly for assistant principals aspiring to become principals. University preparation programs, though vital, are often insufficient in providing assistant principals with comprehensive training (Sun, 2018). These programs typically prepare leaders for principal roles but may not adequately address the unique challenges that lie ahead.

Mentorship necessitates genuine interest and commitment from mentors to guide and support their mentees (Daresh, 2004). It's a reciprocal relationship where both parties invest in mutual growth. However, recent challenges have emerged that have disrupted traditional mentoring dynamics.

CHALLENGES AMPLIFIED BY THE PANDEMIC

The global COVID-19 pandemic, with its shift to virtual learning, has posed significant challenges for educational leaders. The limitations of virtual platforms have hindered the crucial face-to-face connections necessary for effective mentoring (Sincar, 2013). Principals and assistant principals have grappled with the inadequacies of technology in maintaining meaningful connections with staff and students.

Furthermore, gender-related challenges persist within the educational leadership landscape. Female principals often confront distinct obstacles, including biases, marginalization, and scrutiny. Overcoming gender-based stereotypes and expectations becomes an integral part of their leadership journey. Women in leadership positions, irrespective of societal challenges, must mentor both males and females, sharing their experiences and wisdom.

THE THOUGHT

This chapter has delved into the intricate web of politics, accountability, and mentoring challenges within the realm of educational leadership. Education, driven by politics and societal demands, requires adept leaders who can harmonize these forces for the benefit of all stakeholders. Assistant principals aspiring to become principals face a transformative journey, underscored by the realities of leadership.

Accountability, both as a concept and a practice, is central to educational leadership. Principals and assistant principals are not only accountable to stakeholders but also for achieving educational goals, employing available resources efficiently, and adhering to global best practices.

Challenges in mentoring, amplified by the COVID-19 pandemic and gender-related biases, have reshaped the dynamics of leadership development. However, the importance of mentorship remains undiminished, fostering the growth of future educational leaders.

In the ever-evolving landscape of education, understanding and navigating these complexities is essential for educational leaders committed to shaping the future of education. This chapter has provided a comprehensive exploration of the multifaceted challenges and opportunities within the realm of educational leadership, offering insights into the intricacies of this vital field.

CHAPTER 3: RESEARCH METHODOLOGY

This chapter provides a comprehensive insight into the methodology employed to conduct the qualitative study aimed at exploring school administrators' perceptions of best leadership practices and professional development strategies for advancing assistant principals in their careers. The chapter starts by defining the research design, followed by discussions on data collection methods, data interpretation, and the selection and recruitment of participants.

RESEARCH DESIGN

For this study, a qualitative approach was adopted, utilizing Interpretative Phenomenological Analysis (IPA). IPA is a qualitative methodology that delves into detailed examinations of personal lived experiences. It aims to provide a nuanced account of these experiences without being constrained by pre-existing theoretical preconceptions. Instead, IPA focuses on the interpretative aspect of human beings as sense-making organisms. It takes an explicitly idiographic approach, focusing on each case's unique experience before drawing broader conclusions (Smith & Shinebourne, 2012).

In the context of this research, IPA allowed for a deep exploration of the ordinary meaning that school administrators ascribed to concepts or phenomena related to assistant principals' career advancement. The method seeks to describe these meanings by analyzing personal lived experiences from multiple individuals.

RESEARCH QUESTIONS

The study was guided by the following research questions:

1. What do school administrators perceive as the best leadership practices for the career advancement of assistant principals?
2. What do school administrators perceive as professional development strategies for the career advancement of assistant principals?
3. How do principals support their assistant principals through on-the-job training for advancement?

INTERVIEW PROTOCOL

To gather insights from school administrators, an interview protocol was developed. This protocol consisted of 12 open-ended questions for assistant principals, 10 open-ended questions for principals, and seven demographic questions. The questions were designed to align with the research questions and were validated by an expert in the field to ensure their relevance and appropriateness. Closed-ended responses were excluded based on the expert's recommendations.

SETTING

Participants in this study were recruited from a professional educational group on social media. The interviews were conducted via Zoom, allowing for remote participation. Participants were informed that the interviews would be recorded using Zoom's recording system. While participants were encouraged to have their cameras on during interviews for a more personal interaction, it was not mandatory to respect their comfort levels.

SELECTION CRITERIA OF PARTICIPANTS

The participants in this study were public school principals and assistant principals who met

specific criteria. They were required to have a
master's degree or higher and possess a minimum of
3-5 years of experience in their respective positions.
The initial recruitment of participants was carried
out through the LinkedIn professional group named
"Educational Leadership: System and School
Improvement to Increase All Students' Growth and
Achievement." Those who met the criteria and
expressed interest in the study were selected for 45-
minute Zoom interviews. All participants provided
prior consent to record and transcribe the
interviews.

DATA COLLECTION PROCEDURES

Upon receiving approval from the Institutional
Review Board (IRB) at Fayetteville State
University, the data collection process commenced.
Email invitations were sent to selected participants
through LinkedIn, and those who agreed to
participate were sent a consent letter to digitally
sign and return via email. The interviews,
conducted online through Zoom, had an
approximate duration of 45 minutes each. The
interviews aimed to gather rich qualitative data by
allowing participants to reflect on their perceptions
of best practices and professional development

strategies for assistant principals' career advancement.

The interviews were recorded using Zoom's recording feature, and the responses were later transcribed using a digital computer transcription service. The data collection process adhered to ethical guidelines to ensure the rights and privacy of all participants.

DATA ANALYSIS AND INTERPRETATION

The data analysis process followed these key steps:

1. Data Organization: The initial step involved organizing and preparing the data for analysis. This included using a digital computer transcription service to transcribe the narrative data into text.
2. Data Familiarization: The researcher read and reviewed the textual data to gain a preliminary understanding and formulate general ideas.
3. Data Coding: The data was then coded, with the researcher organizing it by marking sections and writing categories in the margins during the coding process.

4. Theme Generation: Categories were further refined into recurring themes for in-depth analysis.
5. Narrative Creation: A narrative was created to describe and elucidate the identified themes.
6. Interpretation: The themes were interpreted in the context of the research questions to provide meaningful insights.

The analysis aimed to identify recurring patterns and themes within the participants' responses, allowing for a deeper understanding of their perceptions and experiences.

DATA STORAGE

To maintain data integrity and confidentiality, several principles were followed:

- Backup copies of computer files were regularly created.
- Zoom recordings and email correspondence related to interviews were securely stored.
- A master list of the types of information gathered was maintained.
- The anonymity of participants was protected by using pseudonyms in the data.

- A data collection matrix was created to visually track and identify information related to the study.

TRUSTWORTHINESS

Ensuring the trustworthiness of the research findings is crucial in qualitative research. Several measures were taken to enhance the credibility of this study. These measures included providing detailed accounts of all responses and data from participants, obtaining informed consent, and maintaining transparency throughout the research process.

SUMMARY

In this chapter, we have explored the methodology employed in this qualitative study. By employing Interpretative Phenomenological Analysis (IPA), the study aimed to delve deep into school administrators' perceptions of leadership practices and professional development strategies for advancing assistant principals' careers. The research design, interview protocol, data collection procedures, analysis process, and ethical considerations have all been outlined, providing a

comprehensive understanding of the methodology
used in this study.

CHAPTER 3: METHODOLOGY

In this chapter, a comprehensive delineation of the research methodology employed for this qualitative study is presented. The central aim of this investigation revolves around the elucidation of school administrators' viewpoints concerning optimal leadership practices and indispensable professional development strategies, with a particular emphasis on their implications for the career progression of assistant principals. This chapter initiates with a delineation of the selected research design, followed by extensive discourse concerning the methodologies governing data collection, interpretation, and the scrupulous selection and recruitment of participants.

RESEARCH DESIGN

The research design underpinning this study is rooted in the qualitative paradigm and harnesses the potency of Interpretative Phenomenological Analysis (IPA). Noteworthy for its capacity to conduct nuanced examinations of personal lived experiences, IPA endeavors to uncover an unadulterated narrative of these experiences, unshackled from preconceived theoretical constructs. Central to the IPA approach is the acknowledgment of humans as inherently sense-making entities. It staunchly adheres to an explicitly idiographic stance, wherein each individual's experience is exhaustively scrutinized before venturing into broader generalizations (Smith & Shinebourne, 2012).

The selection of IPA as our methodological framework aligns seamlessly with our research objectives, given its inherent capacity to explore intricate, often nebulous, and emotionally charged subjects. The intent is to unearth the commonplace meanings interwoven with the experiences of a diverse cadre of individuals, specifically, school administrators.

RESEARCH QUESTIONS

Our research endeavors are underpinned by the following pivotal research inquiries:

1. What are the perspectives of school administrators concerning the most effective leadership practices that facilitate the advancement of assistant principals in their careers?

2. How do school administrators conceptualize professional development strategies in the context of propelling the career trajectories of assistant principals?

3. In what manners do principals contribute to the on-the-job training and support mechanisms intended to foster the advancement of their assistant principals?

INTERVIEW PROTOCOL

The bedrock of our data collection endeavors rests upon a meticulously crafted interview protocol. This protocol comprises two distinct sets of inquiries, tailored to suit the roles of assistant principals and principals, complemented by a set of demographic queries. These questions have been judiciously designed to harmonize with our research goals and the elucidation of research inquiries. To ensure the robustness and pertinence of the protocol, an expert in the field subjected it to a stringent validation process. This meticulous scrutiny led to the curation of a question set devoid of closed-ended queries, in alignment with the recommendations offered by the expert.

SETTING

The locus of our research activities
materialized within the precincts of a professional
educational group ensconced within a prominent
social media platform. The conduits for our data
collection efforts materialized through the
utilization of Zoom, a ubiquitous virtual
communication platform. Participants were
proactively apprised of the recording mechanism
intrinsic to Zoom interviews. Furthermore, they
were apprised of the optional nature of activating
their cameras during the interviews. This latitude
was extended to facilitate the capture of nuanced
facial expressions and non-verbal cues.

SELECTION CRITERIA OF PARTICIPANTS

Our study cohort comprises individuals holding
the roles of public school principals and assistant
principals, and they were meticulously vetted
against specific eligibility criteria. These criteria
encompassed the possession of a master's degree or
higher and a tenure of no less than 3-5 years within
their respective roles. Initial outreach to prospective
participants was executed via the LinkedIn
professional group known as "Educational
Leadership: System and School Improvement to

Increase All Students' Growth and Achievement." Those who met the stipulated criteria and expressed interest were subsequently selected to participate in 45-minute Zoom interviews. Crucially, all participants furnished their informed consent for the utilization of audio recordings and the employment of digital computer transcription services for interview transcriptions.

DATA COLLECTION PROCEDURES

The initiation of our research endeavors was predicated on the receipt of requisite approval from the Institutional Review Board (IRB) at Fayetteville State University, a vital instrument for upholding the rights and privacy of our participants. The commencement of our data collection activities involved the transmission of email invitations to a pre-selected cohort of participants conforming to our eligibility criteria. The recruitment process was predominantly executed within the domain of the professional networking platform, LinkedIn. Our research scope transcended geographical boundaries, adhering to the phenomenological tradition as delineated by Creswell (2013). Interviews constituted the principal modality for data acquisition, proffering a tapestry of rich and comprehensive qualitative data. We embraced the

semi-structured interview format, guided by an
interview protocol meticulously tailored for this
purpose (Creswell, 2007). These interviews,
facilitated through the Zoom platform, provided
participants with an avenue for introspection
concerning their experiences, perceptions of best
practices, and strategies germane to professional
development within the realm of educational
leadership. The active engagement of assistant
principals, given their extant roles, enriched the
research with pertinent insights.

Upon securing the green light from the
Institutional Review Board (IRB) at Fayetteville
State University (refer to Appendix A for specifics),
we compiled a roster of potential participants
sourced from LinkedIn. A judicious selection
process was employed, targeting 45 to 50
individuals meeting our stipulated criteria.
Subsequently, invitations to partake in the study
were extended. To ensure the alignment of our
research practices with ethical standards and to
facilitate informed participation, each participant
was furnished with a digital consent letter, to be
duly executed and returned via email. All interviews
were meticulously recorded using the Zoom
platform, and the resultant audio recordings were

transcribed with scrupulous precision through the employment of a digital computer transcription service. Each interview session adhered to a consistent timeframe of approximately 45 minutes.

DATA ANALYSIS AND INTERPRETATION

Our approach to data analysis and interpretation adhered to a structured sequence of activities:

- Data Organization and Preparation: The initial phase entailed the meticulous organization and preparation of data, with the utilization of a digital computer transcription service to transmute the interview narrative data into textual form.
- Data Familiarization: A comprehensive immersion in the textual data facilitated the formulation of initial general insights.
- Data Coding: Employing a systematic coding process, data segments were categorized, with annotations and categories being methodically affixed within the margins.
- Theme Generation: The categories thus constructed were then synthesized into

recurring thematic elements, forming the
bedrock of our analysis.

- Narrative Construction: The culmination of
  our analysis witnessed the crafting of a
  narrative expounding upon the identified
  themes.
- Interpretation: A rigorous interpretative
  exercise ensued, wherein the themes were
  subjected to meticulous examination within
  the context of our research queries, yielding
  profound insights into the central tenets of
  our study.
- Identification of Recurring Patterns:
  Harnessing the coding process, we discerned
  recurring patterns and thematic elements
  that resonated across participants' responses.
- Characterization and In-Depth
  Interpretation: The final step encompassed
  the characterization of these themes within
  our narrative, accompanied by a profound
  interpretation of the data vis-à-vis our
  research objectives (Creswell, 2013).

Throughout these analytical phases, the
preservation of participants' confidentiality
remained paramount. While diligently safeguarding
their anonymity, we presented the outcomes of our

data analysis in a manner that showcased common recurrent themes. These overarching themes encapsulated diverse facets, spanning perceived obstacles and challenges encountered by principals and assistant principals within public school settings, their distinctive viewpoints, best practices, strategic approaches, the salience of mentorship, and the tactics instrumental to their career advancement. This multi-dimensional analysis aimed to enrich our comprehension of how participants perceived their roles in the realm of education, the reverberations of their experiences on their vocational trajectories, and the strategies they deemed efficacious for their professional advancement.

DATA STORAGE

Our approach to data storage conformed rigorously to the tenets stipulated by Creswell (2013), encompassing:

- Systematic creation of backup copies for all computer files.
- Meticulous archiving of Zoom interview recordings and the preservation of email correspondence germane to these interviews.

- Compiling a master list cataloging the various types of information amassed.
- Diligent safeguarding of participants' confidentiality by the employment of pseudonyms within the data.
- Establishment of a comprehensive data collection matrix, a visual tool facilitating the identification and organization of pertinent information for the study.

TRUSTWORTHINESS

The attainment of trustworthiness in qualitative research is a sine qua non. To this end, we instituted a slew of measures:

- A commitment to rendering comprehensive accounts of all responses and data furnished by participants.
- The diligent acquisition of informed consent from all participants.
- The unwavering commitment to transparency across every phase of the research trajectory.

These measures served as bulwarks fortifying the credibility of our study, in consonance with the principles articulated by McCroskey and Young (1981) concerning the perceiver's assessment of the communicator's knowledge, honesty, and good intentions.

SUMMARY

In this chapter, we have meticulously elucidated the methodological underpinnings of our qualitative study. By embracing the Interpretative Phenomenological Analysis (IPA) methodology, we aspired to glean profound insights into the perspectives of school administrators regarding leadership practices and professional development strategies, with a particular emphasis on the career advancement of assistant principals. We have delineated the research design, interview protocol, data collection procedures, analytical processes, ethical considerations, and data storage methodologies that have underpinned our research endeavor. This comprehensive exposition furnishes a lucid comprehension of the meticulous methodologies employed in our research, positioning us to unearth invaluable insights into the dynamic sphere of educational leadership.

CHAPTER 4: RESULTS OF FINDINGS

This chapter presents the results of a qualitative study employing Phenomenological Analysis (IPA) that delves into the leadership experiences of 10 assistant principals and seven principals in the field of education. Their insights hold significance in the context of promoting accountability and equity for assistant principals aspiring to ascend to the position of a principal. The voices of these school administrators resonate across districts, emphasizing the need for ensuring fair and equal opportunities for those aspiring to occupy leadership roles within the educational landscape.

RESEARCH PURPOSE

The primary objective of this study is to elucidate the perceptions of school administrators regarding best leadership practices and professional development strategies conducive to the career advancement of assistant principals. The overarching aim is to investigate the measures that school districts should undertake to foster a professional culture of mentorship, thereby transcending the confines of nepotism and the age-old adage, "it's not who you know but what you know." The data collection process for this study encompassed 17 interviews conducted via Zoom and WebEx platforms, utilizing Otteri.ai for recording and transcription services.

RESEARCH QUESTIONS

The research inquiry hinged upon the following pivotal questions:

What do school administrators perceive as best leadership practices for the career advancement of assistant principals?

What do school administrators perceive as professional development strategies for the career advancement of assistant principals?

How do principals support their assistant principals through on-the-job training for advancement?

DESCRIPTION OF ASSISTANT PRINCIPAL PARTICIPANTS

The study featured a cohort of assistant principals, each bringing a unique set of experiences and qualifications to the table:

Assistant Principal 1: Serving as an administrator for 2 years, currently a middle school teacher with an educational background in Elementary Education and Sociology, complemented by a master's degree in school administration.

Assistant Principal 2: Possessing 2 years of administrative experience, currently serving as a middle school assistant principal. Holding an undergraduate degree in Business Administration and a master's degree in Executive Leadership, with 11 years of prior teaching experience.

Assistant Principal 3: With 3 years of administrative tenure, currently an assistant principal in a high school. Equipped with an undergraduate degree in Elementary Education and a master's degree in school administration, boasting 13 years of classroom teaching experience.

Assistant Principal 4: Boasting 9 years as an administrator, this individual serves as a middle school assistant principal. Holding an undergraduate degree in Elementary Education and Special Education, complemented by a master's in administration, with 7 years of prior classroom teaching experience.

Assistant Principal 5: A seasoned administrator with 19 years of experience, currently in the role of a high school assistant principal. Possessing an undergraduate degree in music and a master's degree in school administration, with prior teaching roles spanning Band, Chorus, and music appreciation.

Assistant Principal 6: Serving as an administrator for 5 years, this individual holds the position of a middle school assistant principal. Armed with an undergraduate degree in Elementary Education and a Masters in School Administration, with 2 years of prior classroom teaching.

Assistant Principal 7: With 3 years of administrative experience, currently an assistant principal in a middle school. Holding an undergraduate degree in Speech-Theater/Communications and a master's degree in school administration, with 9 years of prior classroom teaching.

Assistant Principal 8: Boasting 5 years as an administrator, this individual serves as a high school assistant principal. Holding an undergraduate degree in Elementary Education and certifications in Middle Grades Social Studies and Reading Education. They earned a doctorate in educational leadership, further strengthening their qualifications.

Assistant Principal 9: With 3 years of administrative tenure, this individual currently serves as a high school assistant principal. Possessing an undergraduate degree in Elementary Education and a master's degree in school administration, with 13 years of classroom teaching experience.

Assistant Principal 10: An administrator with 7 years of experience, currently serving as an assistant principal for grades Pre-K-8. Holding an undergraduate degree in Science Education, a Master of School Administration, and a Doctorate in Educational Leadership. With 23 years of prior teaching experience, this assistant principal has held roles in various educational settings.

DESCRIPTION OF PRINCIPAL PARTICIPANTS

Complementing the cohort of assistant principals are the principals who contributed to this study:

Principal 1: With 16 years of administrative experience, currently serving as a principal for grades 6–8. Holding an undergraduate degree in Spanish Education, a Master of School

Administration (MSA), and a Doctorate in Educational Leadership, with 4 years of prior classroom teaching experience.

Principal 2: Also possessing 16 years of administrative tenure, this principal currently leads a K-5 school. Holding an undergraduate degree in History Education, an MSA, and a Doctorate in Educational Leadership, with 4 years of prior classroom teaching experience.

Principal 3: With 13 years of administrative experience, this principal serves grades PK-5. Holding an undergraduate degree in history and an MSA, with 7 years of prior classroom teaching experience.

Principal 4: Boasting 10 years as an administrator, this individual currently serves as a principal for grades 9th-12th. Holding an undergraduate degree in Speech & Theater and an MSA, with 12 years of prior classroom teaching experience.

Principal 5: With a remarkable 25 years of administrative experience, this individual currently holds the role of Kindergarten Readiness Coordinator for Smart Start. Armed with an undergraduate degree in Elementary Education, an

MSA, and a Doctorate in Educational Leadership, this principal has previously taught grades 5–6 and has led various districts, including the Northeastern Piedmont region.

Principal 6: Serving as an administrator for 15 years, this principal currently holds the position of Executive Director of Federal Programs. Holding an undergraduate degree in Education and Middle Grades, along with an MSA, this principal brings 7 years of prior classroom teaching experience to the table.

Principal 7: With 20 years of administrative experience, this individual currently serves as a principal for grades Pre-K-5th. Possessing an undergraduate degree in History Education, an MSA, and a Doctorate in School Leadership, with 6 years of prior classroom teaching experience.

INTERVIEW PROCESS

The interview process was conducted in a confidential, one-on-one, semi-structured format. A comprehensive interview protocol was employed, encompassing seven demographic questions for both assistant principals and principals, alongside 12 open-ended questions for assistant principals and 10 for principals. These interviews were conducted via virtual platforms, ensuring privacy and comfort for the participants. The researcher conducted the interviews individually, fostering an environment conducive to candid responses.

Furthermore, as a professional courtesy and to enhance the accuracy, credibility, and validity of the findings, participants were given the opportunity to review their responses post-interview. This practice aimed to ensure that their perspectives and experiences were accurately captured.

Throughout the interview process, the enthusiasm and eagerness of the participants were evident. Many participants acknowledged the significance of this study, highlighting the loneliness they sometimes felt in their leadership roles and the importance of self-care. Principals expressed their commitment to mentoring their assistant principals, a duty they deemed essential. Assistant principals, on the other hand, emphasized the pivotal role that principals play in their journey toward principalship, often referring to the influence of politics in this trajectory.

As the researcher, it was imperative to remain neutral throughout the interview process, refraining from interjecting personal narratives. The research topic was informed by the researcher's own experiences as an assistant principal aspiring to become a principal. Therefore, objectivity and a commitment to capturing the unfiltered experiences of the participants were paramount.

DATA ANALYSIS AND THEMES

The analysis of the data involved the identification of recurring themes based on the responses of the participants to the interview questions. Not all responses were included in the findings, but rather those that directly addressed the research questions. The thematic analysis commenced with responses from the assistant principals.

THEMES AND RESPONSES FROM ASSISTANT PRINCIPALS

Interview Question 1: Why did you become an Assistant Principal?

Impact Education on a Larger Scale: The participants' motivations to become assistant principals coalesced around the theme of "Impact Education on a Larger Scale." They expressed a desire to extend their sphere of influence beyond the classroom, aiming to reach more students and teachers through administrative roles. The position of assistant principal afforded them the opportunity to share their knowledge and experiences acquired through educational journeys.

For instance, Assistant Principal 1 articulated, "I wanted to be a leader and to take the knowledge I obtained from my educational experiences, and to apply to the schools as an AP." Similarly, Assistant Principal 5 remarked, "The only way up is to become a principal, go through an administration program. I decided that I wanted to have more responsibility, move up, and take responsibility."

Interview Question 2: What strategies does your district have in place to prepare Assistant Principals for Principalship?

Monthly Cohort Collaboration: The strategies implemented by districts to prepare future building administrators converged on the recurring theme of "Monthly Cohort Collaboration." Assistant principals elaborated on their districts' initiatives, which encompassed mentoring, hands-on training, and professional development. These collaborative platforms facilitated open discussions on school policies, research, and effective leadership strategies.

Assistant Principal 4 explained, "I felt that it would be a good opportunity for me to help more

than just my small part of kids." Assistant Principal
8 emphasized the need for such strategies, stating,
"I want to be a principal one day. I also wanted to
make a larger impact in the school."

This chapter has illuminated the diverse voices
and motivations of assistant principals and
principals, offering a glimpse into their aspirations,
experiences, and the strategies employed by their
districts. The recurring themes underscore the
importance of leadership development and
mentorship, reinforcing the pivotal role that these
school administrators play in shaping the future of
education. The subsequent chapter delves deeper
into the analysis of these themes, providing a
comprehensive exploration of the research findings.

In the dynamic world of education, the role of
assistant principals is crucial in ensuring the smooth
operation of schools. These educators serve as
pillars of support to principals, teachers, and
students, playing multifaceted roles that range from
instructional leadership to student discipline and
community engagement. Preparing to become an
assistant principal, however, is not a journey to be
taken lightly. In this chapter, we delve into the
various avenues that aspiring assistant principals

can explore to equip themselves for this rewarding but demanding role.

LEARNING FROM PEERS: PROFESSIONAL DEVELOPMENT COHORTS

Education is a field that thrives on collaboration and continuous learning. In many school districts, aspiring assistant principals have the opportunity to participate in professional development cohorts. These cohorts often consist of like-minded educators who are looking to take on leadership roles within the district. The experiences within these cohorts can vary based on the number of new principals and the district's specific approach.

Assistant Principal 1 shared insights from their district, where the composition of these cohorts can change based on the number of new principals, sometimes leading to combined cohorts for increased collaboration. The monthly meetings within these cohorts cover a wide range of topics, from school policies to technology training, and even engaging book studies. The collaborative environment fosters a sense of camaraderie among assistant principals, providing them with the support and knowledge they need to excel in their roles.

THE POWER OF PROFESSIONAL DEVELOPMENT

Professional development is the cornerstone of preparing educators for leadership roles. Different school districts employ various strategies to ensure that their assistant principals are well-prepared to navigate the complexities of their roles.

Assistant Principal 2 highlighted the Leader Development Professional Development sessions in their district, which are open to anyone with an administration license or current assistant principals. These sessions offer valuable insights into leadership within the educational context, emphasizing the importance of observing and learning from both effective and struggling teachers. Classroom instruction remains a continuous focus, underscoring its pivotal role in the success of students.

In another district, Assistant Principal 8 shared that they offer Aspiring Assistant Principals leadership workshops, which are tailored for educators with a Masters in School Administration (MSA). Additionally, they have a Leadership Empowerment and Administrator Development (LEAD) program designed to empower and train select assistant principals, preparing them for principal roles. The commitment to nurturing future leaders is evident in these initiatives, as they cover a broad spectrum of disciplines, including leadership, curriculum, instruction, classroom management, and technology.

EQUIPPING FUTURE LEADERS WITH HANDS-ON EXPERIENCE

Beyond classroom learning, practical experience is invaluable for aspiring assistant principals. Assistant Principal 3 emphasized the importance of real-life scenarios and internships. They recounted their experience of an enriching internship where they were entrusted with administrative duties similar to those of an assistant principal or principal. This hands-on approach allowed them to gain invaluable insights into the daily workings of school administration.

Assistant Principal 6 shared their own journey, emphasizing the significance of their internship with a state university's MSA program. This immersive, year-long experience at a middle school provided them with unparalleled hands-on experience, allowing them to function as a leader within the school. This experience was particularly meaningful because it provided a bridge between theory and practice.

FOSTERING LEADERSHIP FROM WITHIN

Many districts recognize the importance of nurturing talent from within their ranks. They provide dedicated programs to groom assistant principals, ensuring they are well-prepared to take on the responsibilities of building-level administrators.

Assistant Principal 9 discussed two leadership programs within their county. The first is a general leadership program open to instructional coaches, assistant principals, and individuals with administrative or second-tier degrees. It offers monthly evening sessions covering various aspects of leadership. The second program is exclusively for assistant principals ready to transition to principal roles. This program, though more selective, offers in-depth instruction on principal leadership.

Assistant Principal 10 revealed an intriguing approach in their district where individuals who have completed the necessary credentials are allowed to shadow other leaders. This shadowing experience provides aspiring leaders with a unique opportunity to learn firsthand from experienced administrators.

THE INVALUABLE ROLE OF MENTORING

Mentorship is a cornerstone of professional growth in the field of education. Assistant principals benefit tremendously from having mentors who guide and support them on their journey toward becoming effective school leaders. Whether it's the experienced principal, a seasoned assistant principal, or a trusted colleague, mentorship provides a safe space to seek advice, ask questions, and gain insights into the nuances of educational leadership.

BEST PRACTICES FOR ASPIRING ASSISTANT PRINCIPALS

In summary, here are some best practices for educators aspiring to become assistant principals:

Seek Hands-On Experience: Actively engage in leadership roles within your school, such as joining the School Improvement Team, taking on department chair positions, or participating in district-level committees. This practical experience is invaluable.

Observe and Learn: Regularly observe teachers across various subjects and grade levels, focusing on both effective and struggling educators. This broadens your perspective on classroom instruction.

Engage in Professional Development: Attend professional development sessions, workshops, and leadership programs offered by your district or educational institutions. These programs cover a wide array of topics critical to educational leadership.

Embrace Internships: If available, consider participating in internships or immersive programs that allow you to experience the daily responsibilities of assistant principals and principals.

Stay Current: Keep yourself updated with the latest trends, research, and best practices in education through reading, networking, and ongoing learning.

Seek Mentorship: Find a mentor or mentors who can guide you on your journey toward leadership. Their experience and advice can be invaluable.

Shadow Experienced Administrators: If possible, take advantage of shadowing opportunities to gain insights into the roles and responsibilities of experienced administrators.

THE CRUCIAL ROLE OF MENTORSHIP IN EDUCATIONAL LEADERSHIP

In the intricate tapestry of educational leadership, mentorship emerges as a guiding light, illuminating the path for those embarking on the challenging journey of an assistant principal. This chapter delves into the profound impact of mentorship, drawing from the experiences and insights shared by the participants in our study. Their narratives not only highlight the multifaceted nature of mentorship but also underscore its pivotal role in shaping effective leaders within the educational domain.

Assistant Principal 1 vividly articulated the significance of mentorship in nurturing leadership potential. For them, mentorship was more than just guidance; it was the catalyst that kindled their confidence as they ventured into the realm of school leadership. Their mentor, a seasoned principal, played a pivotal role in empowering them to step into the role of an instructional leader. Through their mentor's support and guidance, they discovered that leadership transcends mere administrative duties; it is about fostering the growth of teachers, students, and the entire educational community.

Mentorship, as Assistant Principal 2 expounded, extends the horizons of learning for emerging leaders. It equips them with the vital skills needed to evaluate effectively, to be receptive to diverse ideas, and to adapt gracefully to the ever-evolving educational landscape. Mentorship, in this sense, becomes a crucible in which leaders refine their understanding of the intricacies of educational leadership, forging a disposition that can adeptly navigate the complexities and challenges that lie ahead.

Assistant principals, as they embark on their leadership journey, do not merely receive guidance; they acquire a profound understanding of effective leadership through the actions, wisdom, and mentorship of their experienced counterparts. Assistant Principal 3 shared their experiences of transitioning from theoretical understanding to practical application, a transformation facilitated by their mentor. Mentorship, in this context, becomes an immersive experience, offering emerging leaders the invaluable opportunity to observe and absorb leadership in action.

However, the role of mentorship is not confined to the initial stages of leadership. Even seasoned leaders, like Assistant Principal 4, continue to derive immense value from mentorship. In the dynamic and ever-evolving educational arena, where challenges metamorphose and new paradigms emerge, the guidance of a mentor remains an invaluable asset. Access to a mentor's wealth of experience and wisdom offers leaders the opportunity to fine-tune their strategies, adapt to emerging trends, and stay ahead in the ever-changing landscape of education.

Assistant Principal 5 articulated how mentorship has been akin to a mosaic of experiences for them. As they have worked under different principals, each with their unique approach to leadership, they have gained a diverse array of mentorship experiences. This diversity has enriched their leadership journey, endowing them with a broader perspective that allows them to adapt to varying contexts and challenges. Their mentors, therefore, have provided not only guidance but also insights into avoiding pitfalls and anticipating potential challenges.

The multi-faceted nature of mentorship comes to the forefront in Assistant Principal 6's account. They have cultivated a network of mentors, each contributing to their growth in different facets of leadership. A spiritual mentor serves as an anchor, grounding them in moments of reflection and providing solace in the often intense world of education. An educational mentor offers practical advice and strategies, equipping them to navigate the intricacies of classroom management and curriculum development. Simultaneously, a district-level mentor provides insights into the broader educational landscape, helping them understand policy dynamics and navigate administrative challenges. This diversified mentorship network ensures a well-rounded growth experience, preparing them comprehensively for the multifaceted role of an assistant principal.

In essence, mentorship is not a one-size-fits-all endeavor; it is a dynamic and adaptive relationship. It tailors itself to the unique needs, aspirations, and challenges faced by each leader. Moreover, its benefits extend beyond the administrative sphere. Assistant Principal 7 insightfully noted that mentorship has played a significant role in their journey, not only as an educational leader but also as an individual. Through mentorship, they have learned not only the intricacies of running a school but also the importance of maintaining personal well-being, resilience, and emotional intelligence.

Mentorship is a continuous and evolving journey. It commences with the building of confidence, navigates through the intricacies of leadership, and provides a lifeline during challenging times. It fosters resilience, enables self-reflection, and bolsters leaders in their quest to create meaningful and impactful educational experiences. The experiences and insights shared by the participants in this study underscore the indispensable role mentorship plays in the realm of educational leadership. It is a vital thread that weaves wisdom, guidance, and support into the complex and ever-evolving landscape of education, ensuring that emerging and seasoned leaders alike are well-equipped to meet the demands of their roles effectively.

The significance of mentorship is perhaps best encapsulated by the words of Assistant Principal 8, who noted that mentorship has been fundamental to their success as an educational leader. It has not only assisted them in making informed decisions but has also equipped them with the confidence and knowledge needed to navigate the multifaceted challenges of the educational realm. As the educational landscape continues to evolve, mentorship remains a steadfast source of guidance,

wisdom, and support for leaders dedicated to
shaping the future of education.

FOSTERING PERSONAL AND PROFESSIONAL GROWTH

In the intricate tapestry of educational
leadership, the nurturing of personal and
professional growth stands as an essential thread.
This chapter delves into the perceptions of how
principals attend to the multifaceted development of
assistant principals. Within this tapestry, a recurring
theme emerges: the principal's role in fostering the
individual growth of their assistant principals.
Participants shared insights into how their
principals, recognizing the uniqueness of each
leader, facilitated a holistic journey of development.

THE DUAL FACETS OF GROWTH

Participants identified two fundamental
dimensions of growth: personal and professional.
They affirmed that these aspects are intrinsically
intertwined, and effective leaders are those who
understand the delicate balance between them.

Assistant Principal 1 elucidated how their
principal approached this duality. By encouraging
volunteerism and offering opportunities for teachers
to sponsor clubs, a nurturing environment for

personal growth was created. Simultaneously, professional growth was attended to through administration evaluations, providing feedback that aided not only in their development but also in aligning their goals with the school's broader objectives.

Assistant Principal 3 echoed this sentiment, sharing how their principal emphasized aligning personal and professional goals with student success. This alignment, they believed, was pivotal in crafting a well-rounded leader capable of driving educational excellence.

THE OPEN-DOOR POLICY

Several assistant principals emphasized the significance of their principal's open-door policy. Assistant Principal 4 highlighted that this accessibility fostered an environment where professional development suggestions were openly discussed. This dialog allowed for the identification of growth opportunities that resonated with each leader individually.

Assistant Principal 5 emphasized how their principal's open-door policy extended beyond the professional realm. The principal inquired about their well-being, demonstrating a commitment to the assistant principal's personal life. This holistic approach to leadership development acknowledged that personal challenges could impact professional effectiveness.

SUPPORTING INDIVIDUAL CIRCUMSTANCES

Assistant Principal 7 shared a profound insight into their journey. Their principal had an astute ability to analyze their needs, focusing on areas that required attention to propel them to the next level. This tailored approach to development ensured that leadership skills were honed in areas of greatest impact.

ENABLING ASPIRATIONS

For Assistant Principal 8, the journey into leadership was marked by unwavering support from their principal. Both personal and professional growth were prioritized, with transparency and commitment to their development. This unfaltering support fortified their journey into educational leadership.

NAVIGATING THE PATH TO LEADERSHIP

The ascent to the role of assistant principal is a journey shaped by diverse experiences and trajectories. In this chapter, we explore the distinct career paths undertaken by our participants, shedding light on the varied backgrounds that converge in educational leadership.

THE CLASSROOM ODYSSEY

Many of our participants embarked on their leadership journey from the classroom. Assistant Principal 1 shared their experiences teaching across different grade levels, from third and fourth grade to middle school subjects. This foundational classroom experience provided them with a profound understanding of the core of education – the students.

Assistant Principal 2 followed a similar trajectory. Their career spanned various teaching roles, from being a High School BED TA to a Middle School PE teacher and ultimately a High School Business Teacher and CDC/SPC instructor. This rich diversity of roles nurtured a well-rounded perspective on education.

THE PATH THROUGH COACHING

Assistant Principal 3 carved their path through instructional coaching, investing heavily in curriculum development and data analysis. This unique journey equipped them with a comprehensive grasp of instructional intricacies, a skill set invaluable for a leader in educational administration.

THE PRINCIPAL FELLOWS PROGRAM

Assistant Principal 4 embarked on their journey after completing the NC Principal Fellows program. Their background in special education, coupled with experience as a SpEd facilitator and Curriculum Facilitator, laid a strong foundation for leadership.

THE INFLUENCE OF A SUPPORTIVE PRINCIPAL

Assistant Principal 5's trajectory was deeply influenced by the perceptive leadership of their principal. Recognizing their potential, their principal encouraged them to explore the path of educational administration. This transition from a dedicated teacher to an instructional leader was marked by the pursuit of an MSA degree.

THE TRANSITION FROM MENTORING TO LEADERSHIP

Assistant Principal 6 began as a fifth-grade teacher and then ventured into mentoring students. The internship became a pivotal phase, allowing them to shift their focus towards leadership development. Experiences such as MTSS coordination and involvement in athletics and testing broadened their leadership skill set.

FROM TEACHER ASSISTANT TO LEADER

Assistant Principal 7's journey commenced as a teacher assistant and bus driver. Their ascent was marked by a relentless pursuit of roles with increasing responsibilities. Understanding the value of building effective teams, they embarked on a mission to surround themselves with capable individuals, a hallmark of effective leadership.

THE EVOLUTION OF AN INSTRUCTIONAL LEADER

Assistant Principal 8's journey spanned from being a classroom teacher to a grade-level chair. This progression continued through roles as a Science Lab teacher and Instructional Coach. These diverse experiences allowed them to evolve into an educational leader, capable of providing system-wide professional development.

The diverse journeys narrated in this chapter exemplify the multifaceted nature of educational leadership. While each path is unique, they collectively contribute to the rich mosaic of leadership that shapes the landscape of education.

In the intricate fabric of educational leadership, decisions are the threads that weave the path towards transformation. In this chapter, we explore the methods through which principals engage their assistant principals and staff in the decision-making process. The ability to solicit ideas, take calculated risks, and nurture a culture of collaboration emerges as the defining hallmark of effective leadership.

FOSTERING OPEN DIALOGUE

A recurring theme among our participants is the importance of open dialogue. Assistant Principal 1 underscores this by highlighting the channels through which teachers at their school can communicate ideas and concerns. A Google doc, continuously updated and reviewed by the principal and APs, serves as an avenue for immediate feedback and problem-solving. This transparent approach empowers teachers and staff to play an active role in decision-making.

Assistant Principal 2 echoes the sentiment, emphasizing how their principal delegates duties, thereby making teachers more accountable. Daily meetings with the administrative staff serve as a platform for soliciting ideas and feedback. This inclusive approach ensures that decisions are rooted in the collective wisdom of the school community.

EMBRACING DIVERSITY OF THOUGHT

Assistant Principal 3 highlights a key aspect of their principal's leadership - a willingness to embrace diversity of thought. The principal recognized the value of having an assistant principal with a contrasting perspective. This dynamic duo, with their distinct viewpoints, strengthens the decision-making process by fostering balanced, well-informed choices.

ENCOURAGING RISK-TAKING

Risk-taking is a hallmark of dynamic leadership, and our participants attest to this quality in their principals. Assistant Principal 4 describes how their principal actively encourages risk-taking. Through dialogue and discussion, ideas are presented, examined, and sometimes rejected. This process, far from stifling innovation, cultivates an environment where calculated risks are not just accepted but celebrated.

INCORPORATING STAFF IDEAS

Assistant Principal 5 shares their experience of a principal who values staff input. Ideas, whether they concern bulletin boards or significant technology investments, find a place in the decision-making process. This approach fosters a sense of ownership and engagement among the staff, creating a shared vision that drives the school forward.

PASSION AND EXCELLENCE

Assistant Principal 7 provides insights into their principal's leadership style, characterized by passion and a commitment to excellence. The principal sets high expectations and is unafraid to challenge conventions when it serves the best interests of the students. This unwavering focus on what is best for children defines the decision-making ethos of the school.

INCLUSIVE DECISION-MAKING STRUCTURES

Assistant Principal 9 discusses the importance of structured decision-making processes. The School Improvement Team plays a pivotal role in shaping decisions. Weekly admin meetings and grade-level meetings provide avenues for different types of decisions, ensuring a comprehensive approach to school management.

LEARNING FROM STUDENT DEMONSTRATIONS

In a unique scenario, Assistant Principal 10 describes how their principal turned a student demonstration into a learning experience. When students sought to express themselves regarding mask mandates, the principal saw it as an opportunity to engage students in a structured and safe demonstration. This adaptive leadership approach showcases the willingness to harness unforeseen situations for the benefit of student growth and understanding.

This chapter helps us witness the art of collaborative decision-making as practiced by these educational leaders. The ability to create channels for input, encourage risk-taking, and prioritize the best interests of students form the core of their leadership philosophy. This ethos, threaded through their decision-making fabric, propels their schools towards educational excellence.

CULTIVATING MENTORSHIP AND EFFECTIVE COMMUNICATION

In the intricate landscape of educational leadership, mentorship and effective communication are the cornerstones upon which successful leadership is built. In this chapter, we delve into the strategies employed by principals to serve as mentors and coaches to their assistant principals while nurturing open channels of communication.

LEADING BY EXAMPLE: A COMMON THREAD

One resounding theme emerges from the wisdom shared by these principals: leading by example. As Principal 1 emphasizes, actions speak louder than words. This principle is foundational in building trust, respect, and pride among assistant principals and staff. It starts with understanding the nuances of the school community and taking time to listen. Principals invest energy in getting to know their teams personally, acknowledging individual interests, and identifying common ground.

Transparency becomes the bedrock upon which trust is built, as Principal 2 asserts. Principals open the door to personal conversations, sharing their own likes, dislikes, and interests. This candidness fosters a culture of honesty and openness, crucial for effective mentorship.

PERSONALIZED COACHING APPROACHES

Principal 1 employs a multifaceted approach to mentorship. This includes the Model-Teach-Practice coaching method, where strengths and areas of improvement are discussed. This method not only reinforces skills but also instills a sense of pride in accomplishments.

Additionally, these leaders actively engage in dialogue with their assistant principals. Regular one-on-one conversations provide opportunities for mentors to gauge progress, lend support, and offer encouragement. This ongoing dialogue ensures that assistant principals feel valued, heard, and supported.

BUILDING BRIDGES THROUGH COMMUNICATION

Open and empathetic communication remains a cornerstone of these mentorship approaches. Principal 3 highlights the importance of asking simple yet profound questions like "How do you feel?" and "Are you facing any challenges?" These inquiries serve as a reminder that leaders are

invested in the well-being and professional growth
of their assistant principals.

Principal 6 underscores the value of honesty
and collaboration. Leaders and their teams are
partners, working together to overcome challenges.
Mentorship doesn't exist in a vacuum; it thrives
within a context of mutual respect and shared
commitment.

INVESTING IN PROFESSIONAL GROWTH

Principal 4 exemplifies a structured approach to
mentorship. Goals are collaboratively set, standards
are established, and progress is regularly monitored.
This systematic approach ensures that the
mentorship journey is guided by clear objectives,
fostering a sense of direction and achievement.

Additionally, these leaders emphasize the
importance of continuous learning and professional
development. They provide opportunities for
assistant principals to attend workshops,
conferences, and training sessions to enhance their
skills and knowledge. This investment in
professional growth not only benefits the
individuals but also strengthens the entire school
leadership team.

ENCOURAGING ASPIRATIONS AND CHALLENGING GROWTH

A recurring thread among these leaders is the encouragement of aspiring to higher positions. Principal 5 explicitly conveys the expectation that assistant principals should aim for principal roles. This aspiration, coupled with the challenge to constantly improve, fuels professional growth. It fosters an environment where administrators are not just content but eager to develop and make a meaningful impact.

Principal 7 echoes this sentiment, emphasizing the importance of leadership development programs and succession planning. These initiatives identify and nurture future leaders within the organization, ensuring a seamless transition when leadership roles become available.

CREATING A SUPPORTIVE ATMOSPHERE

Beyond coaching and mentoring, these leaders actively work to create a supportive atmosphere within their schools. Principal 6 describes the importance of teamwork and unity. Leaders are not isolated figures but integral parts of a collaborative effort. They actively engage with their teams, participate in school activities, and demonstrate their commitment to the school's mission and values.

Additionally, several principals describe their commitment to fostering a sense of family and belonging within the school community. Principal 1 highlights the importance of building teacher leadership and involving staff in shaping the school's mission and vision. When individuals feel a sense of ownership and pride in their school's direction, they become more invested in its success.

REFLECTING AND ADAPTING

Finally, mentorship is not a one-size-fits-all endeavor. Leaders like Principal 7 acknowledge the importance of adaptability. Each assistant principal may have unique needs and preferences, requiring mentors to tailor their guidance and support accordingly. Mentorship is not a static process but a dynamic exchange that evolves to meet the needs of both mentors and mentees.

In this chapter, we witness the transformative power of mentorship and effective communication in educational leadership. Principals who lead by example, prioritize open dialogue, personalize coaching approaches, invest in professional growth, encourage aspirations, and create supportive atmospheres forge lasting partnerships that drive educational excellence. These mentorship journeys are not just professional relationships but enduring collaborations that shape the leaders of tomorrow.

NAVIGATING THE LONELY LANDSCAPE OF EDUCATIONAL LEADERSHIP

In the realm of educational leadership, traversing the complex terrain of public schools presents a myriad of challenges. In this chapter, we delve into the personal reflections of principals as they candidly discuss the trials and tribulations they encounter in their roles.

LEADERSHIP: A LONELY JOURNEY

An undeniable truth surfaces throughout these interviews - leadership can be a profoundly solitary pursuit. Principal 1 aptly describes it as "lonely" and underlines the weight of expectations that come with the role. This solitude emerges from being the lynchpin of an educational ecosystem, where myriad stakeholders look to principals for guidance, solutions, and support.

The multifaceted nature of leadership leaves principals juggling various roles. They must wear the hats of counselors, instructors, leaders, and mentors, all while balancing the delicate scales of sanity and balance. Yet, Principal 1 remains undaunted, always seeking opportunities for self-improvement and growth. This relentless pursuit of excellence fuels the resilience necessary for this lonely journey.

CHALLENGES IN AN EVER-CHANGING LANDSCAPE

The landscape of public education is in constant flux, with new challenges emerging frequently. The COVID-19 pandemic has accentuated the need for adaptable leadership. Principal 2 highlights the dramatic rise in student dropouts during the pandemic, an issue that thrusts educational leaders into unprecedented territory. Managing the fallout from such crises is a testament to the resilience of these leaders.

Equity is another cornerstone issue in public education, as underscored by Principal 4. Navigating the delicate balance between academic rigor and ensuring equitable opportunities for all students presents a persistent challenge. Administrators must push teachers to engage all students, acknowledging that each child brings unique experiences and value to the classroom.

DIVERSITY AND LEADERSHIP

Principal 5 brings attention to a fundamental issue - the underrepresentation of females and minorities in educational leadership roles. Historically, the image of a school principal has been that of a white male. This perception poses an extra layer of challenge for women and individuals from minority backgrounds who continually strive to prove their qualifications and competence in leadership roles.

Overcoming these stereotypes and biases necessitates an unwavering commitment to breaking down barriers. Leaders like Principal 5 are pioneers, demonstrating that leadership knows no gender or ethnicity, and that great decisions are the outcome of competence, not gender.

BALANCING ACT: POLITICS AND PERSONAL LIFE

The challenges of leadership extend into the realm of politics and personal life. Principal 6 underscores the formidable role politics plays in educational leadership. Navigating the intricate web of political dynamics while staying steadfast in the commitment to providing an adequate education for every student is a high-wire act. The need to balance the demands of work and personal life adds

another layer of complexity to this leadership
journey.

FINDING SOLACE AND SUPPORT

In the face of these formidable challenges,
finding solace and support becomes paramount.
Principals require safe spaces where they can vent
frustrations, share concerns, and seek guidance.
Principal 3 highlights the importance of mentorship
that goes beyond merely identifying areas of
improvement. Effective mentors offer constructive
counsel and build mentees' capacity to address
shortcomings without crushing their spirits.

Furthermore, Principal 4 stresses the
significance of finding thought partners, even
outside one's immediate school community. These
trusted colleagues offer opportunities for
collaborative growth and problem-solving.

NAVIGATING THE PATH AHEAD

In this chapter, we have glimpsed into the trials
and triumphs of educational leadership in public
schools. The path is undeniably challenging, and the
landscape ever-changing. Yet, the resilience,
dedication, and unwavering commitment of these
leaders shine through.

As we conclude this exploration, it's essential to recognize that while the road may be solitary, it is not insurmountable. Leaders like those featured here are forging ahead, breaking down barriers, and ensuring that the future of education is brighter for all students, regardless of their background or circumstance. The challenges of leadership are many, but so are the rewards, and it is through the collective efforts of dedicated leaders that these challenges can be overcome.

SUPPORT AND LEADERSHIP DEVELOPMENT FOR PRINCIPALS

Interview Question 5: If you could implement support for yourself and other leaders, what would that look like?

Support and ongoing professional development are essential for leaders in the education field. Principals often find themselves in challenging and isolated roles. To effectively support themselves and other leaders, the following strategies were discussed:

PRINCIPAL 1: BUILDING PROFESSIONAL LEARNING COMMUNITIES

Principals should have access to support groups or professional learning communities where they can debrief, unwind, and ask questions.

Networks should be established to facilitate the sharing of concerns and best practices.

Professional development opportunities should focus on key areas of leadership, such as instruction, finance, and HR.

PRINCIPAL 3: ADDRESSING SOCIAL-EMOTIONAL HEALTH

Support should extend beyond professional development to include a focus on leaders' social and emotional well-being.

The workplace should be a place where leaders desire to be, which requires a supportive and healthy environment.

Flexibility in the form of support is crucial to accommodate the various burdens and responsibilities leaders carry, including family responsibilities.

PRINCIPAL 6: PERSONAL WELLNESS AND GROWTH

Support for leaders should include opportunities for personal wellness check-ins.

Leaders need opportunities to receive support, just as they provide support to others.

Creating a balance between work and personal life is essential for the well-being of leaders.

PRINCIPAL 7: TAILORED PROFESSIONAL DEVELOPMENT

Professional development for leaders should be tailored to their specific needs and challenges.

Instead of implementing one-size-fits-all approaches, districts should conduct surveys to identify the most relevant training topics.

Avoid following trends blindly; focus on providing relevant and impactful support.

Interview Question 6: What strategies does your district have in place to prepare future building administrators?

The preparation of future building administrators is crucial to ensure a pipeline of effective leaders in the education system. Several strategies were mentioned:

PRINCIPAL 1: ASPIRING PRINCIPALS PROGRAM

The district has an "aspiring principals program" that selects a group of assistant principals through an application and interview process.

The program provides workshops on key leadership areas, including finance, HR, and instruction.

It concludes with mock interviews to help candidates become familiar with the process.

PRINCIPAL 2: PROFESSIONAL DEVELOPMENT AND AN ACADEMY

The district offers professional development opportunities for assistant principals.

An academy specifically targets assistant principals to prepare them for future principal roles.

PRINCIPAL 3: LEADERSHIP SEMINARS AND WORKSHOPS

The district organizes leadership seminars and workshops, allowing current educators and administrators to interact with district leaders and experts.

These opportunities identify potential future leaders who demonstrate leadership skills.

Principal 4: Support from External Organizations

An organization called New Leaders supports assistant principals in the district.

New Leaders offers professional development to build the capacity of assistant principals to become effective principals.

Principal 5: Assistant Principal Leadership Institute

The district has established an Assistant Principal Leadership Institute.

Monthly meetings focus on topics relevant to preparing assistant principals for principal roles.

Assistant principals have the opportunity to apply what they learn in their schools.

Principal 6: Monthly Assistant Principal Professional Development

Assistant principals participate in monthly professional development opportunities.

These sessions include guest speakers, activities, and collaboration among assistant principals.

The district ensures continuous growth and learning for assistant principals.

PRINCIPAL 7: PROGRESSIVE TRAINING PROGRAMS

In more progressive districts, there are intentional processes for growing young leaders.

These programs allow potential leaders to interact with district leadership and receive training.

The goal is to prepare future leaders and identify potential candidates for leadership roles.

Interview Question 7: How do you feel your years in leadership prepare you for a building-level administrator?

Experience is a valuable teacher, and years in leadership roles provide essential preparation for building-level administrators:

PRINCIPAL 1: LEARNING BY DOING

Gained valuable experience by participating in various programs and workshops.

Highlights the importance of learning by doing and the need for professional networks.

Describes how a supportive mentor helped prepare for the principal role.

PRINCIPAL 2: LEADERSHIP AND TEACHING EXPERIENCE

Years of experience in leadership and teaching roles helped develop leadership skills.

Being a team leader in the classroom and working with diverse personalities prepared for leadership.

Emphasizes the need to understand and empathize with various perspectives.

PRINCIPAL 3: LEARNING FROM MISTAKES

Acknowledges the role of making mistakes in the learning process.

Shares an example of a scheduling mistake and how it led to improvement.

Reflects on the importance of having leadership that understands the learning curve.

PRINCIPAL 4: GUIDANCE FROM SUPPORTIVE PRINCIPALS

Describes a principal who actively mentored and coached during the assistant principal role.

Learning by shadowing the principal's actions and decision-making.

Being prepared through guidance and practical experience.

PRINCIPAL 5: PREPARATION THROUGH TEACHING EXPERIENCE

Teaching experience in the classroom prepared for understanding students' and teachers' needs.

Recognizes that the transition to the principal role requires a different perspective.

Emphasizes the importance of adapting leadership skills to the broader school context.

PRINCIPAL 7: PROGRESSIVE DISTRICT TRAINING

Years of experience in progressive districts helped in understanding leadership.

Points out the challenge of transitioning from secondary to elementary leadership.

Highlights the importance of humility and a willingness to learn new aspects of education.

In summary, the strategies and experiences shared by these principals underscore the significance of ongoing support, tailored professional development, and practical experience in preparing leaders for building-level administrative roles in the education field. Building a strong foundation through mentorship and learning by doing is essential for effective leadership.

In this comprehensive exploration, we delve deeply into the multifaceted realm of professional development strategies and leadership practices designed to propel assistant principals toward career advancement. Drawing upon the candid insights shared by a diverse array of participants, including seasoned principals and other seasoned educational administrators, we unearth the fundamental principles that underscore the creation of effective educational leaders in the dynamic landscape of contemporary schools.

NETWORKING THROUGH COLLABORATION: A FUNDAMENTAL IMPERATIVE

The resonating theme of networking through collaboration stood tall amidst the participants' responses. Principals and seasoned administrators unanimously underscored the critical role of teamwork, mentorship, and collaboration in fostering career growth among assistant principals. This collective wisdom underscored the simple truth that leadership is not an insular endeavor; rather, it thrives within an ecosystem of collaboration, mentorship, and consistent professional development.

Principal 1, whose weekly administrative meetings and multifaceted task assignments highlighted the importance of collaborative experiences, articulated that enabling assistant principals to navigate various responsibilities was central to their professional development. This approach not only nurtured their skills but also honed their ability to thrive in diverse leadership roles.

Principal 2, echoing this sentiment, accentuated the necessity of empowering assistant principals to self-assess their areas of improvement while actively engaging them in school affairs. This approach laid the foundation for future leadership by dispelling the notion of leadership as an exclusive club and emphasizing that every team member's input holds value.

Principal 3, by offering assistant principals opportunities to attend district-provided professional development, illuminated the power of exposure and experience. By simulating a principal's responsibilities and progressively exposing assistant principals to this multifaceted role, they were prepared for the challenges and opportunities that awaited them in their leadership journey.

Principal 4, recognized the importance of professional development, both within and outside the district. The significance of ensuring that assistant principals actively participated in these opportunities to broaden their knowledge base and enhance their leadership competencies was profoundly emphasized.

Principal 5, however, approached the concept of networking through collaboration from a slightly different angle. Leveraging data, particularly the teacher working condition survey, was a central component of identifying areas requiring additional development. Through this data-driven approach, professional development initiatives were tailored to address specific needs, ensuring a laser-focused approach to career growth.

Principal 6, took inclusivity in leadership to heart. By including assistant principals in essential school decisions, from day-to-day operations to being consistently copied on school-related correspondence, the path towards leadership was made smoother. The intentional avoidance of relegating assistant principals to mere "grunt" work underscored a commitment to their growth and development.

SUPPORT FOR LEADERSHIP PROGRESSION: THE GUIDING LIGHT

A cornerstone theme that emerged from the rich tapestry of insights was the pivotal role of mentoring and coaching in supporting the leadership progression of assistant principals. The participants emphasized that consistent mentoring and coaching are not mere tools but rather guiding lights illuminating the path toward becoming an effective school leader.

CHALLENGING, TAKING RISKS, AND SOLICITING IDEAS: THE POWER OF OPEN DIALOGUE

The final theme that resonated was the strategies employed to challenge, take risks, and solicit ideas from assistant principals when making decisions for the school. In this context, clear and consistent lines of communication emerged as the linchpin for achieving effective leadership.

Principal 1, enlightened us with the concept of delegation, coupled with a coaching approach. It was made clear that fostering an environment where assistant principals feel empowered to contribute their ideas is essential. This approach allows them to share their visions, refine them collaboratively, and execute them effectively.

Principal 2, emphasized the creation of a culture characterized by teamwork and open dialogue. Within this construct, assistant principals are encouraged to participate actively in discussions and decision-making processes. This open forum fosters trust and mutual respect.

Principal 3, described a gradual approach to exposing assistant principals to challenging situations. This immersion helps them gain insights into decision-making processes and progressively expands their leadership capacities.

Principal 4, detailed the importance of weekly meetings to discuss expectations and empower assistant principals to present their ideas. The collaborative discussions that follow enable refining decision-making skills and fostering a sense of ownership.

Principal 5, astutely recognized the necessity of giving voice to resource executive teachers, who often feel overlooked amidst the focus on content teachers. Incorporating their concerns and ideas into decision-making ensures a more comprehensive approach to leadership.

Principal 6, advocated for open communication and collaboration through regular discussions and joint problem-solving. This ongoing dialogue equips assistant principals with the decision-making skills necessary for effective leadership.

Principal 7, brought to the forefront the principle of "Disagree but Commit." It emphasizes the importance of open communication, even in situations of disagreement. This principle ensures that once a decision is made, everyone commits to it, fostering unity and progress.

CONCLUSION: UNIFYING THREADS OF LEADERSHIP DEVELOPMENT

In conclusion, this chapter has unveiled a tapestry of leadership development strategies that resonate deeply with the experiences of educational leaders. The unifying threads weaving through these strategies are mentorship, collaboration, communication, and consistent professional development. Each strategy, while distinct, is interconnected with the others, creating a holistic framework for nurturing future educational leaders.

As we delve deeper into this exploration, it becomes increasingly evident that these strategies are not standalone; they form a symbiotic relationship, each reinforcing the others. The roadmap to effective leadership development hinges on a comprehensive approach that integrates mentorship, professional growth opportunities, and inclusive decision-making processes. These findings offer valuable guidance for educators, administrators, and policymakers seeking to cultivate leadership excellence within their educational ecosystems.

In the forthcoming chapters, we will delve further into the practical implications of these strategies. Real-world examples and best practices will serve as beacons guiding educational leaders committed to advancing the careers of their assistant principals and, by extension, enhancing the quality of education within their schools.

CHAPTER 5: DISCUSSION, IMPLICATIONS, AND RECOMMENDATIONS

The transition from a classroom teacher to an assistant principal is often assumed to involve no significant change in professional identity. This transition is often undertaken with minimal preparation, inadequate induction, and a lack of structured training or tools to assess the processes of change involved. While numerous studies have focused on the tasks and preparedness of assistant principals for promotion to the principal role, there is limited research specifically addressing the entry phase into the assistant principal role—a pivotal stage in one's managerial career.

This qualitative study delves into the perspectives of public school principals and assistant principals regarding effective leadership practices and strategies for the advancement of assistant principals. It also explores the guidelines implemented within school districts to facilitate the professional growth of assistant principals aspiring to become principals. This chapter summarizes the key findings of the study and offers recommendations for future research, all within the framework of the Transformational Leadership Model.

STUDY OVERVIEW

The study employed an Interpretative Phenomenological Analysis (IPA) methodology to investigate the viewpoints of assistant principals and principals concerning mentorship, principalship, and the expectations inherent to their leadership roles. IPA allowed for the collection of diverse perspectives and experiences, which were subsequently analyzed to extract collective meanings.

STUDY PROCEDURES

Data were gathered through semi-structured interviews with ten assistant principals and seven principals currently serving in leadership roles. These assistant principals had each transitioned from classroom teaching roles and held positions as instructional leaders for over three years in grades K-12.

SUMMARY OF FINDINGS

The interviews revealed several recurring themes, which were discussed from the perspectives of both assistant principals and principals. The core themes revolved around the importance of mentorship in leadership roles and the urgent need for districts to facilitate these conversations, adequately prepare assistant principals, and offer ongoing mentorship and coaching.

INTERPRETATION OF PARTICIPANTS' RESPONSES

Q1. What are the school administrators' perceptions of best practices and professional development strategies for the career advancement of assistant principals?

SEVERAL THEMES EMERGED:

1. Impact Education on a Larger Scale: Assistant principals sought the principalship role to have a greater impact on education at a systemic level. They aimed to address student and teacher needs, ensuring instructional success and academic achievement.

2. Monthly Cohort Collaborations: Assistant principals highlighted the importance of structured collaboration within a cohort. This collaborative

environment was seen as beneficial for mentorship and building self-efficacy, which is critical for developing leadership skills.

3. Hands-On Experience is Vital: Hands-on experience was deemed essential in the journey to becoming effective leaders. Involvement in decision-making, professional development, and instructional coaching were seen as key components.

4. Observing and Shadowing the Principal: Shadowing principals was considered crucial for acquiring leadership skills. Assistant principals valued opportunities to observe and learn from their principals, particularly in dealing with stakeholders.

5. Learning Loss Due to COVID: The COVID-19 pandemic presented substantial challenges in education. Learning loss, digital literacy, and staff shortages were discussed, emphasizing the pivotal role of leadership during crises.

6. The Professional Obligation of Mentorship: Mentorship was highlighted as a professional obligation. Building positive relationships with principals, attending professional development, and participating in mentorship programs were essential for assistant principals' growth.

7. The Purpose of Mentorship: Mentorship was recognized as a means of developing leadership skills. Effective mentors were described as knowledgeable, supportive, reliable, and trustworthy.

8. Differentiating Professional and Personal Growth: Districts and principals were noted for their support of both professional and personal growth. Feedback, coaching, and self-assessment were considered valuable in this process.

9. Traditional Approach to Leadership: Assistant principals' classroom experience was seen as beneficial for their roles as instructional leaders. Having served as classroom leaders before becoming administrators was regarded as valuable.

10. The Principal Provides Leadership Opportunities: Principals were viewed as crucial in articulating the school's vision and fostering staff buy-in. They achieved this through team-building, data-driven decision-making, and transparent leadership.

11. Promoting Open-Door Policy and Solicits Input: Principals encouraged open communication and sought input from their teams. Collaboration,

active listening, and team engagement were seen as essential components of leadership.

12. Providing Effective Strategies: Effective leadership involved providing strategies to enhance teaching and learning. Principals leveraged book studies, surveys, and relationship-building to create a supportive environment.

13. Leading by Example: Principals were expected to lead by example. They demonstrated leadership through their actions, setting clear expectations, and promoting a positive school culture.

14. Progression Towards Leadership Goals: Leadership development involved participating in leadership cohorts, mentoring, and coaching programs. The journey toward leadership goals required continuous learning and support.

15. Supportive Environment for Growth: Building self-efficacy and creating a supportive environment were crucial for assistant principals' confidence and success.

16. Challenges in Education as a Leader: School leaders faced various challenges, including the loneliness of leadership, student dropout rates,

and political hurdles that hindered equitable
education.

17. Monthly Professional Learning
Community: Professional development and
networking opportunities within a community of
peers were considered essential for leadership
growth.

18. Leadership Preparatory Process: The
preparatory process was essential for equipping
principals for their roles. Leadership cohorts,
mentoring, and intentional development contributed
to successful outcomes.

19. Networking Through Collaboration:
Collaborative networking with peers and mentors
played a significant role in leadership development.

20. Mentorship and Coaching Goals: Effective
mentorship and coaching should be transparent,
trust-based, and goal-oriented. Mentors were
expected to provide support and guidance.

21. Consistent Lines of Communication: Open
communication and consistent feedback were
highlighted as essential components of leadership.

IMPLICATIONS FOR CHANGE

The findings of this study carry several implications for change within educational leadership:

1. Equity and Diversity in Leadership: Districts should prioritize equity and diversity in leadership positions, ensuring that mentorship and development opportunities are accessible to all aspiring leaders.

2. Transformational Leadership Focus: Mentorship and leadership development should emphasize not only transactional leadership but also transformational leadership qualities. This shift will contribute to more effective and inspirational leadership.

3. Transparent Conversations: Encourage open and transparent conversations between principals and assistant principals regarding career advancement and mentorship. This promotes clarity of purpose and mutual understanding.

4. Structured Mentorship Programs: Establish structured mentorship programs that provide clear objectives, guidance, and support for assistant principals. These programs should align with leadership standards.

5. Ongoing Leadership Development:
Continuously invest in the leadership development
of assistant principals. Monthly professional
learning communities and networking opportunities
can enhance their skills and knowledge.

6. Addressing Challenges: Acknowledge the
challenges faced by school leaders, such as
isolation, student dropout rates, and political
obstacles. Develop strategies to overcome these
challenges collectively.

RECOMMENDATIONS FOR FUTURE RESEARCH

To further explore the dynamics of educational
leadership and mentorship, future research
endeavors may include:

1. Equity and Hiring Practices: Investigate
districts' hiring practices and their impact on
equitable leadership representation.

2. Methodological Variation: Replicate this
research using different research methodologies to
gain a deeper understanding of leadership
experiences.

3. Superintendent Perspectives: Expand the
study to include superintendents and associate

superintendents to explore their career paths and the benefits of mentoring for career advancement.

4. Diversity and Marital Status: Examine the influence of marital status and diversity on leadership experiences and effectiveness.

CONCLUSION

This study underscores the significance of mentorship, professional development, and structured leadership programs for assistant principals transitioning to principalship roles. Through the lens of the Transformational Leadership Model, it reveals the intricate web of relationships and experiences that shape the professional identities and effectiveness of educational leaders. By implementing the recommendations and addressing the implications for change, educational institutions can better prepare their leaders to navigate the challenges and complexities of modern education. In doing so, they contribute to the creation of a more equitable, innovative, and student-centered educational landscape.

REFERENCES

Akbari, T. T., & Pratomo, R. R. (2021). The new normal leadership: How technology alter communication style in contemporary organization. *Jurnal Komunikasi Ikatan Sarjana Komunikasi Indonesia*, *6*(1), 1–12.

Alsarayareh, R. S., Al-khasawneh F. M., & Al Soub, T. F. (2022). Parental engagement in online teaching and learning during COVID-19 pandemic: Implications for sustainable education. *Journal of Teacher Education for Sustainability*, *24*(1), 129–144. https://doi.org/10.2478/jtes-2022-0010

Allensworth, E., Huang, H., & Sebastian, J. (2016). The role of teacher leadership in how principals influence classroom instruction and student learning. *American Journal of Education*. Retrieved from http://www.journals.uchicago.edu/t-and-c

American Psychiatric Association. (1994). *Diagnostic and statistical manual of mental disorders* (4th ed.). American Psychiatric Association.

Anderson, R. E., & Dexter, S. L. (2000). *School technology leadership: Incidence and impact.* Centre for Research on Information Technology and Organizations. University of California. Retrieved from http://www.crito.uci.edu/tlc/findings/report_6/report_6.pdf

Argon, T. (2015). Teacher and administrator views on school principals' accountability. *Educational Sciences: Theory & Practice*, *15*(4), 925–944. https://doi.org/10.12738/estp.2015.4.2467

Armstrong, D. E. (2015). Listening to voices at the educational frontline: New administrations' experiences of the transition from teacher to assistant principal. *Brock Education Journal*, *24*(2), 109–122.

Avolio, B. J. (2007). Promoting more integrative strategies for leadership theory-building. *The American Psychologist*, *62*, 25–33.

Avolio, B. J., Waldman, D. W., & Yammarino, F. J. (1991). Leading in the 1990s: The four I's of transformational leadership. *Journal of European Industrial Training, 15*(4), 9–16.

Avolio, B. J., & Yammarino, F. J. (2002). *Transformational and charismatic leadership: The road ahead.* Elsevier Science.

Baig, L. A., Ali, S. K., & Sarfaraz, S. (2022). Role of politics, guilds and pedagogy in defining policies in medical education: The Pakistan scenario. *Pakistan Journal of Medical Sciences, 38*(6), 1708–1713. https://doi.org/10.12669/pjms.38.6.6057

Baker, B. D., & Cooper, B. S. (2005). Do principals with stronger academic backgrounds hire better teachers? Policy implications for

improving high-poverty schools.

Educational Administration Quarterly,

41(3), 449–479.

https://doi.org/10.1177/0013161X04269609

Bandura, A. (1977). Self-efficacy: Toward a

unifying theory of behavioural change.

Psychological Review, *84*, 191–215.

Bandura, A. (1986). *Social foundations of thought

and action: A social cognitive theory.*

Prentice-Hall.

Bandura, A. (1997). *Self-efficacy: The exercise of

control.* W. H. Freeman.

Bass, B. M. (1985). *Leadership and performance

beyond expectations.* Free Press.

Bass, B. M. (1990). From transactional to transformational leadership: Learning to share the vision. *Organizational Dynamics, 18*(3), 19–31. https://doi.org/10.1016/0090-2616(90)90061-s

Bass, B. M., & Riggio, R. E. (2010). The transformational model of leadership. In G. R. Hickman (Ed.), *Leading organizations: Perspectives for a new era* (2nd ed., pp. 76–86). Sage.

Bass, B. M., Avoilio, B. J., Jung, D. I., & Berson, Y. (2003). Predicting unit performance by assessing transformational and transactional leadership. *Journal of Applied Psychology, 88*(2), 207–218.

Bass, B. M. (2008). *The Bass handbook of leadership: Theory, research, and managerial applications* (4th ed.). Free Press.

Bass, B. M. (1995). Theory of transformational leadership redux. *Leadership Quarterly, 6*(4), 463–78

Bearman, S., Blake-Beard, S., Hunt, L., & Crosby, F. J. (2007). New directions in mentoring. In T. D. Allen & L. T. Eby (Eds.), *The Blackwell handbook of mentoring: A multiple perspectives approach* (pp. 375–396). Blackwell.

Bennis, W. G. (2003). *On becoming a leader* (Rev. ed.). Basic Books.

Bennis, W. (2007). The challenge of leadership in the modern world: Introduction to special issues. *American Psychologist, 62*, 2–5. https://doi.org/10.1037/0003-066X.62.1.2

Béteille, T., Kalogrides, D., & Loeb, S. (2012). Stepping stones: Principal career paths and school outcomes. *Social Science Research, 41*(4), 904–919. https://doi.org/10.1016/j.ssresearch.2012.03.003

Bickmore, T., & Cassell, J. (2001). *Relational agents: A model and implementation of building user trust.* ACM CHI 2001 Conference Proceedings, Seattle, WA. Retrieved from

http://www.media.mit.edu/gnl/publications/r

eaSmalllTalkchi2001.pdf

Bond, L., Carlin, J. B., Thomas, L., Rubin, K., &

Patton, G. (2001). Does bullying cause

emotional problems? A prospective study in

young teenagers. *British Medical Journal*,

323, 4804.

Bovens, M. A. P. (2007). Analysing and assessing

accountability: A conceptual framework.

European Law Journal, *13*(4), 447–468.

https://doi.org/10.1111/j.1468-

0386.2007.00378.x

Branch, G. F., Hanuschek, E. A., & Rivkin, S.

(2013). School leaders matter: Measuring

the impact of effective principals. *Education*

Next, *13*, 1–8.

https://www.educationnext.org/school-leaders-matter/

Brown v. Board of Education. (2022). Retrieved from https://www.history.com/topics/black-history/brown-v-board-of-education-of-topeka

Bryk, A. S., & Schneider, B. (2002). *Trust in schools: A core resource for improvement.* Russell Sage Foundation.

Buckner, J. C. (1988). The development of an instrument to measure neighborhood cohesion. *American Journal of Community Psychology, 16*(6), 771–791. https://doi.org/10.1007/BF00930892

Burkhauser, S., Gates, S. M., Hamilton, L. S., & Ikemoto, G. S. (2012). *Challenges and opportunities facing principals in the first*

year at a school. RAND Corporation.

Retrieved from

https://www.rand.org/pubs/research_briefs/

RB9643.html

Burns, J. M. (1978). *Leadership.* Harper & Row

Castillo-Montoya, M. (2016). Preparing for

interview research: The interview protocol

refinement framework. *The Qualitative*

Report, 21(5), 811–831.

https://nsuworks.nova.edu/tqr/vol21/iss5/2

Cherry, K. (2019). *Autocratic leadership.* Retrieved

from https://www.verywellmind.com/what-

is-autocratic-leadership-2795314

Chickering, A. W. (1969). *Education and identity.*

Jossey-Bass.

Clark, K. E., & Clark, M. B. (Eds.). (1990).

Measures of leadership. Leadership Pr Ltd.

Cohen, R., & Schecter, C (2019). *Becoming an*

assistant principal: Mapping that facilitates

or hinder entering the role. Retrieved from

https://files.eric.ed.gov/fulltext/EJ1218851.p

df

Covey, S. (2004). *The 8th habit.* Free Press.

Cranston, N., Tromans, C., & Reugebrink, M.

(2004). Forgotten leaders: What do we know

about the deputy principalship in secondary

schools? *International Journal of*

Leadership in Education, 7, 225–242.

Creswell, J. W. (2007). *Qualitative inquiry and*

research design: Choosing among five

approaches (3rd ed.). Sage.

Creswell, J. W. (2013). *Qualitative inquiry & research design: Choosing among five approaches* (3rd ed.). Sage.

Danielson, C. (2002). *Enhancing student achievement: A framework for school improvement.* Association for Supervision and Curriculum Development.

Daresh, J. (2004). Mentoring school leaders: Professional promise or predictable problems? *Educational Administration Quarterly, 40*(4), 495–517. https://doi.org/10.1177/0013161X04267114

Day, C., & Johansson, O. (2008). Leadership with a difference in schools serving disadvantaged communities: Arenas for success. In K. Tirri

(Ed.), *Educating moral sensibilities in urban schools* (pp. 19–34). Sense Publishers.

Day, D. (2011). Leadership development. In A. Byrman, D. Collinson, K. Grint, B. Jackson, & M. Uhl-Bien (Eds.), *The SAGE handbook of leadership* (pp. 37–50). SAGE.

Day, C., Gu, Q., & Sammons, P. (2016). The impact of leadership on student outcomes: How successful school leaders use transformational and instructional strategies to make a difference. *Educational Administration Quarterly, 52*(2), 221–258. https://doi.org/10.1177/0013161X15616863

de Haan, E., & Duckworth A. (2012). The coaching relationship and other common factors in executive coaching outcome. In E. de Haan

& C. Sills (Eds.), *Coaching relationships: The relational coaching field book* (pp. 185–196). Liberi.

de Moura, G. (2020). *Cybersecurity leadership principles: Lessons learnt during the covid-19 pandemic to prepare for the new normal.* World Economic Forum, Não Convencional, Homeland Security Digital Library.

De Pree, M. (1989). *Leadership is an art.* Bantam Doubleday Dell.

Department for Professional Employees. (2019). *School administrators: An occupational overview.* Fact Sheet 2019. https://static1.squarespace.com/static/5d10ef48024ce300010f0f0c/t/5e2f2b1864fffb0e24

35f9c0/1580149529043/School+Administrat

ors+Fact+Sheet+2019.pdf

Dicke, T., Marsh, H. W., Parker, P. D., Guo, J.,

Riley, P., & Waldeyer, J. (2020). Job

satisfaction of teachers and their principals

in relation to climate and student

achievement. *Journal of Educational*

Psychology, 112(5), 1061–1073.

https://doi.org/10.1037/edu0000409

Dimmock, C. (2012). *Leadership, capacity building*

and school improvement: Concepts, themes

and impact. Routledge

Educational Research Service. (2000). *The*

principal, keystone of a high-achieving

school: Attracting and keeping the leaders

we need. Arlington, VA.

Einarsen, S. (1999). The nature and causes of bullying at work. *International Journal of Manpower*, *20*(1/2), 16–27.

Ely, K., Boyce, L. A., Nelson, J. K., Zaccaro, S. J., Hernez-Broome, G., & Whyman, W. (2010). Evaluating leadership coaching: A review and integrated framework. *The Leadership Quarterly*, *21*(4), 585–599. https://doi.org/10.1016/j.leaqua.2010.06.003

Elmore, R. F. (2000). *Building a new structure for school leadership.* Albert Shanker Institute.

Evans P. M., & Mohr, N. (1999). Professional development for principals: Seven core beliefs. *Phi Delta Kappan*, *80*(7), 530–532.

Fiedler, F. E. (1971). Validation and extension of the contingency model of leadership effectiveness: A review of empirical findings. *Psychological Bulletin, 76*(2), 128–148. https://doi.org/10.1037/h0031454

Field, T. (1996). *Bully in sight: How to predict, resist, challenge and combat workplace bullying.* Wessex Press.

Fields, L. J. (2002). *The effects of a professional development cadre on new Assistant principals.* Corwin Press.

Fisher, Y. (2014). The timeline of self-efficacy: Changes during the professional life cycle of school principals. *Journal of Educational Administration, 52*(1), 58–83. https://doi.org/10.1108/JEA-09-2012-0103

Fink, S., & Silverman, M. (2014, April). *Principals as instructional leaders.* http://www.sai-iowa.org/Principals-as-instructional-

leaders.pdf

Frazier, K. N. (2011). Academic bullying: A barrier

to tenure & promotion for African-American

faculty. *Florida Journal of Education

Administration & Policy*, 5(1).

https://files.eric.ed.gov/fulltext/EJ961222.pd

f

Frink, D. D., & Klimoski, R. J. (2004). Advancing

accountability theory practice: Introduction

to the human resource management review

special edition. *Human Resource

Management Review*, *14*(1), 1–17.

https://doi.org/10.1016/j.hrmr.2004.02.001

Flanagan, L., & Jacobsen, M. (2003). Technology

leadership for twenty-first century principal.

Journal of Educational Administration,
41(2), 124–142.
https://doi.org/10.1108/09578230310464648

Fleming, K., & Millar, C. (2019). Leadership
capacity in an era of change: the new-
normal leader. *Journal of Organizational
Change Management, 32*(3), 310–319.
https://doi.org/10.1108/JOCM-05-2019-492

Flessa, J. J. (2007). *Poverty and education:
Towards effective action: A review of the
literature.* Ontario Institute for Studies in
Education.

Flauto, F. J. (1999). Walking the talk: The
relationship between leadership and
communication competence. *Journal of
Leadership Studies, 6*(1-2), 86–97.

Francisco, C. D., & Nuqui, A. V. (2020).
Emergence of a situational leadership during
COVID-19 pandemic called new normal
leadership. *Online Submission*, *4*(10), 15–
19.

Frost, L. A., & Kersten, T. (2011). *The role of the
elementary principal in the instructional
leadership of special population.* Retrieved
from
https://files.eric.ed.gov/fulltext/EJ973829.pd
f

Fullan, M. (2001). *Leading in a culture of change*.
Jossey-Bass.

Fullan, M. (2003). *Change forces with a vengeance.*
Routledge & Falmer Press.

Gill, J. (2012). Aspiring principals need fortified programs to prepare them for challenges they face. *Strength Training, 33*(6). Retrieved from www.learningforward.org

Goldring, E., Rubin, M., & Herrmann, M. (2021). *The role of assistant principals: Evidence and insights for advancing school leadership.* The Wallace Foundation. https://www.wallacefoundation.org/knowledge-center/pages/the-role-of-assistantprincipals-evidence-insights-for-advancing-school-leadership.aspx

Goldring, E., Huff, J., May, H., & Camburn, E. (2018). School context and individual characteristics: What influences principal practice? *Journal of Educational*

Administration, 46(3), 332–352.

https://doi.org/10.1108/09578230810869275

Goodson, C. (2000). Assisting the assistant

principal. *Principal, 79*, 56–57.

Gordon, N., & Reber, S. (2020). Federal aid to

school districts during the COVID-19

recession. *National Tax Journal, 73*(3), 781–

804. https://doi.org/10.17310/ntj.2020.3.07

Grint, K. (2011). A history of leadership. In A.

Bryman, D. Collinson, K. Grint, B. Jackson,

& M. Uhl-Bien (Eds.), *The Sage handbook

of leadership.* Sage.

Grissom, J. A., Egalite, A. J., & Lindsay, C. A.

(2021). *How principals affect students and

schools: A systematic synthesis of two*

decades of research. The Wallace Foundation.

Grissom, J. A., Loeb, S., & Master, B. (2013). Effective instructional time use for school leaders: Longitudinal evidence from observations of principals. *Educational Researcher, 42*(8), 433–444.

Grover, K. L. (1994). *A study of first year elementary principals and their mentors in the New York city public schools.* American Research Educational Association.

Hallinger, P., Hosseingholizadeh, R., Hashemi, N., & Kouhsari M. (2017). Do beliefs make a difference? Exploring how principal self-efficacy and instructional leadership impact teacher efficacy and commitment in Iran.

Educational Management Administration & Leadership, *46*(5), 800–819.

https://doi.org/10.1177/1741143217700283

Hattie, J. A. (1992). Measuring the effects of schooling. *Australian Journal of Education*, *36*(1), 5–13.

Halverson, T. J., & Plecki, M. L. (2015). Exploring the politics of differential resource allocation: Implications for policy design and leadership practice. *Leadership and Policy in Schools*, *14*(1), 42–66. https://doi.org/10.1080/15700763.2014.9831 29

Hammer, C., & Gerald, E. (1987). Selected Characteristics of Public and Private School Adminstrators (Principals) (1987-88).

National Center for Education Statistics,
NCES 90-085.

Hartzell, G., William, R., & Nelson, K. (1995,
February). *The influential assistant
principal: Building influence and a stronger
relationship with your principal.* A
Presentation at the 79th Annual Convention
and Exhibit of the National Association of
Secondary School Principals, San Antonio,
Texas. Retrieved from
https://files.eric.ed.gov/fulltext/ED385948.p
df

Harris, A. (2008). *Distributed school leadership:
Developing tomorrow's leaders.* Routledge.

Harris, A., & Spillane, J. (2008). Distributed
leadership through the looking glass.

Management in Education, 22(1), 31–34.

https://doi.org/10.1177/0892020607085623

Hausman, C., Nebeker, A., & McCreary, J. (2001). The worklife of the assistant principal. *Journal of Educational Administration, 40*(2), 136–157.

https://doi.org/10.1108/09578230210421105

Harsh, S., & Casto, M. (2007). Professional codes of ethics: Principles and principals. Retrieved from The Ohio State University, The Principal's Office Web site at http://principalsoffice.osu.edu/files/profreadings.3.08.php

Heffernan, A. (2018). The accountability generation: Exploring an emerging leadership paradigm for beginning principals. *Discourse: Studies in the Cultural Politics of Education, 39*(4), 509–520. https://doi.org/10.1080/01596306.2017.1280001

Hoel, H. (1999). *Workplace bullying: Current state of research.* Employee Health Bulletin.

Hollis, L. (2012). *Bully in the ivory tower.* Patricia Berkly.

Horwood, M., Marsh, H. W., Parker P. D., Guo, J., & Dicke, T. (2021). Burning passion, burning out: The passionate school principal, burnout, job satisfaction, and extending the dualistic model of passion. *Journal of Education Phycology, 113*(8),

1668–1688.

https://doi.org/10.1037/edu0000664

House, R. J. (1977). A 1976 theory of charismatic leadership. In J. G. Hunt & L. L. Larson (Eds.), *Leadership: The cutting edge* (pp. 189–207). Southern Illinois University Press.

Hoyer, K. M., & Sparks D. (2017). *Instructional time for third-and-eighth graders in public school year 2011-2012: Stata in education.* National Center for Education Statistics. https://nces.ed.gov/pubs2018/2018054.pdf

Kaagan, S. S., & Markle, B. W. (1993). Leadership for learning. *Perspective*, *5*(1), 1–16.

Ivey, A. E., Ivey, M. B., & Zalaquett, C. P. (2010). *Intentional interviewing and counseling:*

Facilitating client development in a multicultural society (7th ed.). Brooks/Cole.

Jandrić, P., Knox, J., Besley, T., Ryberg, T., Suoranta, J., & Hayes, S. (2018). Postdigital science and education. *Educational Philosophy and Theory*, *50*(10), 893–899. https://doi.org/10.1080/00131857.2018.1454 000

Jean-Marie, G., & Martinez, A. (2007). Race, gender, & leadership: Perspectives of female secondary leaders. In S. M. Nielsen & M. S. Plakhotnik (Eds.), *Proceedings of the Sixth Annual College of Education Research Conference: Urban and International Education Section* (pp. 43–48).

Kafele, B. (2020, May 16th). *"Your Role is To
Assist not Lead the School" – Virtual AP
Leadership Academy (Week 3).* Retrieved
from
https://www.youtube.com/watch?v=qh01Qk
yki3s

Kalman, M., & Gediklioğlu, T. (2014). An
investigation of the relationship between
school administrators' accountability and
organizational justice. *H. U. Journal of
Education, 29*(2), 115–128.
http://www.efdergi.hacettepe.edu.tr/yonetim
/icerik/makaleler/83-published.pdf

Kantor, H. (2015). *The role of the assistant
principal in leadership transition.*
https://www.nais.org/magazine/independent-

school/spring-2015/the-role-of-the-assistant-principal-in-leadership/

Katz, D., & Kahn, R. L. (1978). *The social psychology of organizations.* Wiley.

Kerns, C. D. (2016). High-impact communication: A key leadership practices. *Journal of Applied Business & Economics, 18*(5).

Kerns, C. D., & Ko, K. (2014). Managerial leadership competencies: A practice-oriented action role framework. *International Leadership Journal, 6*(1), 82–99.

Keashly, L., & Neuman, J. (2010). Faculty experiences with bullying in higher education. *Administrative Theory & Praxis, 32*(1), 48–70.

Kovjanic, S., Schuh, S. C., & Jonas, K. (2013). Transformational leadership and performance: An experimental investigation of the mediating effects of basic needs satisfaction and work engagement. *Journal of Occupational and Organizational Psychology, 86*, 543–555. https://doi.org/10.1111/joop.12022

Kouzes, J. M., & Posner, B. Z. (2016). *Learning leadership: The five fundamentals of becoming an exemplary leader.* Wiley.

Kram, K. (1985). *Mentoring at work: Developmental relationships in organizational life.* Scott Foresman.

Kram, K. E., & Ragins, B. R. (2007). *The handbook of mentoring at work: Theory research & practice.* Sage.

Krug, S. E., Ahadi, S. A., & Scott, C. K. (1991). Current issues and research findings in the study of school leadership. In P. Thurston & P. Zodiates (Eds.), *Advances in educational administration* (Vol. 2). JAI Press.

Kwan, P., & Walker, A. (2011). APs in Hong Kong: Their responsibilities, role alignments, job satisfaction, and career aspirations. In A. R. Shoho, B. Barnett, & A. K. Tooms (Eds.), *Examining the assistant principalship: New puzzles and perennial challenges for the 21st century* (pp. 59–80). Information Age.

Kysburn, U. A., Kalagbor, L., & Harrison A. (2016). The politics of education leadership: Its implications for secondary school improvement in River State. *Journal of Education and Practice*, *7*(21).

Lasater, K. (2016). School leaders' relationships: The need for explicit training on rapport, trust, and communication. *Journal of School Administration Research & Development*, *1*(2).

Lattuca, F. P. (2012). *Becoming an administrator: The socialization of an assistant principal through an autoethnographic lens* (Doctoral dissertation, University of Rhode Island).

Lee, J., Superman, H., & Hastings, L. (2020). The influence of being a mentor on leadership development: Recommendations for curricular & co-curricular experiences. *Journal of Leadership Education, 19*(3), 44–60. https://journalofleadershiped.org/wp-content/uploads/2020/07/19_3_Lee.pdf

Leithwood, K., & Louis, K. S. (2012). *Linking leadership to student learning.* Jossey-Bass.

Leithwood, K., Day, C., Sammons, P., Harris, A., & Hopkins, D. (2006). *Successful school leadership: What it is and how it influences pupil learning.* DfES.

Leithwood, K., Harris, A., & Hopkins, D. (2008). Seven strong claims about successful school leadership. *School Leadership & Management, 28*(1), 27–42. https://doi.org/10.1080/13632430701800060

Leymann, H. (1990). Mobbing and psychological terror at workplaces. *Violence and Victims*, 5(2), 119–126. Retrieved from https://pubmed.ncbi.nlm.nih.gov/2278952/

Levinson, D. J., Darrow, C. N., Klein, E. B., Levinson, M. H., & McKee, B. (1978). *The seasons of a man's life.* Ballantine Books.

Liu, S., Huang, J. L., & Wang, M. (2014). Effectiveness of job search interventions: A meta-analytic review. *Psychological Bulletin, 140*, 1009–1041. https://doi.org/10.1037/a0035923

Lipson, J. G. (1994). Ethical issues in ethnography. In J. M. Morse (Ed.), *Critical issues in qualitative research methods* (pp. 333–355). Sage.

Lockwood, A. L., Evans, S., & Eby, L. T. (2010). Reflections on the benefits of mentoring. In T. D. Allen & L. T. Eby (Eds.), *The Blackwell handbook of mentoring: A multiple perspectives approach* (pp. 233–236). Blackwell.

Lowstuter, C., & Robertson, D. P. (1995). *Network your way to your next job–fast.* McGraw-Hill

Malone, B. G., Sharp, W., & Thompson, Jr., J. C. (2000). *The Indiana principalship: Perceptions of principals, aspiring principals, and superintendents.* Paper presented at the annual meeting of the Midwestern Educational Research Association, Chicago, IL.

Marshall, C. (1992). The assistant principalship: An

overview of the frustrations, rewards.

NASSP Bulletin, 76(547), 88–94.

https://doi.org/10.1177/01926365920765471

1

Marshall, C., & Hooley, R. M. (2006). *The assistant*

principal: Leadership choices and

challenges. Corwin.

Marshall, C., & Phelps Davidson, E. (2016). As

assistant principals enter their careers: A

case for providing support. *International*

Journal of Mentoring and Coaching in

Education, 5(3), 272–278.

https://doi.org/10.1108/IJMCE-04-2016-

0038

Marzano, R., Waters, T., & McNulty, B. (2005). *School leadership that works.* Association of Supervision and Curriculum Development.

Masten, A. S., & Garmezy, N. (1985). Risk, vulnerability, and protective factors in developmental psychopathology. In B. B. Lahey, & A. E. Kazdin (Eds.), *Advances in clinical child psychology* (Vol. 8, pp. 1–52). Plenum Press.

McCroskey, J. C., & Young, T. J. (1981). Ethos and credibility: The construct and its measurement after three decades. *The Central States Speech Journal, 32*(1), 24–34. https://doi.org/10.1080/10510978109368075

McGrath, J. E. (1962). *Leadership behavior: Some
requirements for leadership training.* U.S.
Civil Service Commission, Office of Career
Development.

Meador, D. (2020). *The role of the principal in
schools.* ThoughtCo. Retrieved from
https://www.thoughtco.com/role-of-
principal-in-schools-3194583

Melton, T. D., Mallory, B. J., Mays, R., & Chance,
L. (2011). Challenges to school leadership
practice. In A. R. Shoho, B. Barnett, & A.
K. Tooms (Eds.), *Examining the assistant
principalship: New puzzles and perennial
challenges for the 21st century* (pp. 81–110).
Information Age.

Melia, M. (2022). Schools with in-person learning scramble for subs: *St. Louis Post-Dispatch*. Retrieved from https://link.gale.com/apps/doc/A688962290/HRCA?u=faye81655&sid=ebsco&xid=93974099

Merrick, L. (2011). *How coaching & mentoring can drive success in your organization.* Retrieved from https://www.coachmentoring.co.uk/assets/How-Coaching-Mentoring-Can-Drive-Success-in-Your-Organization.pdf

Mertz, A. (2006). The organizational socialization of principals. *Journal of School Leadership, 16*, 664–675.

Mertz, N. T. (2000). *Contextualizing the position of assistant principal.* Paper presented at the annual meeting of the University Council for Educational Administration, Albuquerque, NM.

Morgan, T. L. (2014). *Understanding the leadership capacity and practice of assistant principals.* Paper presented at UCEA Convention of the University Council for Educational Administration, Washington, DC.

Mulford, B. (2008). The leadership challenge: Improving learning in schools. *Australian Council for Educational Research, 53*, 1–88. Retrieved from https://research.acer.edu.au/aer/2/

Mumford, M. D., Friedrich, T. L., Caughron, J. J., & Byrne, C. L. (2007). Leader cognition in real-world settings: How do leaders think about crises? *The Leadership Quarterly, 18,* 515–543. https://doi.org/10.1016/j.leaqua.2007.09.002

Murashkin, M., & Tyrväinen, J. (2020). *Adapting to the new normal: A qualitative study of digital leadership in crisis* (Unpublished Master Thesis, Department of Business Administration, Umeå School of Business, Economics and Statistics).

Msila, V. (2014). African leadership models in education: Leading institutions through Ubuntu. *The Anthropologist, 18,* 1105–1114.

Myende, P. E. (2019). Creating functional and sustainable school-community partnerships: Lessons from three South African cases. *Educational Management Administration & Leadership*, *47*(6), 1001–1019. https://doi.org/10.1177/1741143218781070

Naidoo, B., & Perumal, J. (2014). Female principals leading at disadvantaged schools in Johannesburg, South Africa. *Educational Management Administration & Leadership*, *42*(6), 808–824. https://doi.org/10.1177/1741143214543202

National Open University of Nigeria. (2008). *EDA: 755 Responsibility and accountability in education management.* National Open University of Nigeria.

Newby, T., & Corner, J. (1997). Mentoring for

increased performance: Steps in the process.

Performance Improvement, *36*(5), 6–10.

https://doi.org/10.1002/pfi.4140360503

Niedl, K. (1996). Mobbing and well-being:

Economic and personal development

implications. *European Journal of Work and*

Organisational Psychology, *5*(2), 239–249.

https://doi.org/10.1080/13594329608414857

Nicola, M., Alsafi, Z., Sohrabi, C., Kerwan, A., Al-

Jabir, A., Iosifidis, C., Agha, M., & Agha,

R. (2020). The socio-economic implications

of the coronavirus pandemic (COVID-19):

A review. *International Journal of Surgery*,

78, 185–193.

https://doi.org/10.1016/j.ijsu.2020.04.018

Noman, M., & Gurr, D. (2020). Contextual

leadership and culture in education. In G. W.

Nobit (Ed.), *Oxford Research Encyclopedia of*

Education. Oxford University Press

Notar, C. E., Uline, C. S., & Eady, C. K. (2008).

What makes an "effective" leader? The

Application of Leadership. *International*

Education Studies, 1(3), 25–29. Retrieved

from

https://files.eric.ed.gov/fulltext/EJ1065447.p

df

Oleszewski, A., Shoho, A., & Barnett, B. (2012).

The development of assistant principals: A

literature review. *Journal of Education*

Administration, 50(3), 264–286

Oplatka, I., & Tamir, V. (2009). I don't want to be a school head: Women deputy heads' insightful constructions of career advancement and retention. *Educational Management Administration & Leadership*, *37*(2), 216–238.

Özdemir, Y. (2018). The views of prospective teachers on the political context of education & teacher roles in the classroom. *Universal Journal of Education Research*, *6*(11), 2498–2508. https://doi.org/10.13189/ujer.2018.061114

Owen, N. (2015). *Charismatic to the core: A fresh approach to authentic leadership.* SRA Books.

Parlak, B. (2011). *Kamu yönetiminde yeni vizyonlar.* Alfa Aktüel Yayınları.

Panyako, D., & Rorie, L. (1987). The changing role of the assistant principal. *NASSP Bulletin, 71*(501), 6–8. https://doi.org/10.1177/019263658707150103

Pounder, D., & Crow, G. (2005). Sustaining the pipeline of administrators. *Educational Leadership, 62*(8), 56–60. https://eric.ed.gov/?id=EJ725930

Quinn, R. E., & Cameron, K. S. (1988). Paradox and transformation: A dynamic theory of organization and management. In R. E. Quinn & K. S. Cameron (Eds.), *Paradox and transformation: Toward a theory of chance in organization and management.*

Ballinger.

Ramaswami, A., & Dreher, G. (2007). The benefits

associated with workplace mentoring

relationships. In T. D. Allen & L. T. Eby

(Eds.), *The Blackwell handbook of*

mentoring: A multiple perspectives

approach (pp. 211–232). Wiley Blackwell.

Raskauskas, J., & Skrabec, C. (2011). Bullying and

occupational stress in academia:

Experiences of victims of workplace

bullying in New Zealand universities.

Journal of Intergroup Relations, 35(1), 18–

36.

Rayner, C., & Cooper, C. (1997). Workplace

bullying: Myth or reality - can we afford it

ignore it? *Leadership and Organisation*, *18*(4), 211–214. https://doi.org/10.1108/01437739710182313

Read, S. P. (2011). Factors that influence the preparedness of teachers for the vice-principal role. In A. R. Shoho, B. Barnett, & A. K. Tooms (Eds.), *Examining the assistant principalship: New puzzles and perennial challenges for the 21st century* (pp. 11–34). Information Age.

Riggio, R., Riggio, H., Salinas, C., & Cole, E. (2003). The role of social and emotional communication skills in leader emergence and effectiveness. *Group Dynamics, Theory, Research, and Practice, 7*, 83–103.

Riley, P. (2015). *The Australian principal occupational health, safety & well-being survey: 2015 data.* ACU. Retrieved from https://www.healthandwellbeing.org/assets/reports/AU/2018_AU_Final_Report.pdf

Romzek, B. S., LeRoux, K., Johnston, J., Kempf, R. J., & Piatak, J. S. (2014). Informal accountability in multisector service delivery collaborations. *Journal of Public Administration Research and Theory*, *24*, 813–842.

Ryen, A. (2004). Ethical issues. In C. Seale, G. Gobo, J. F. Gubrium, & D. Silverman (Eds.), *Qualitative research practice* (pp. 230–247). Sage.

Rubin, H. J., & Rubin, I. S. (2012). *Qualitative
interviewing: The art of hearing data* (3rd
ed.). Sage.

Rutter, M. (1987). Psychosocial resilience and
protective mechanisms. *American Journal of
Orthopsychiatry*, *57*, 316–331.
https://doi.org/10.1111/j.1939-
0025.1987.tb03541.x

Savickas, M. L. (2007). Career adaptability: An
integrative construct for life-span. *Life-
Space Theory*, *45*(3), 247–259.
https://doi.org/10.1002/j.2161-
0045.1997.tb00469.x

Sahu, P. (2020). Closure of universities due to
coronavirus disease 2019 (COVID-19):
Impact on education and mental health of

students and academic staff. *Cureus*, *12*(4),

e7541. https://doi.org/10.7759/cureus.7541

Şahın, S. (2004). The relationship between

transformational and transactional

leadership styles of school principals and

school culture (The case of Izmir, Turkey).

Kuram ve Uygulamada Eğitim Bilimleri,

4(2), 387–395.

Schiller, J. (2003). Working with ICT: Perceptions

of Australian principals. *Journal of

Educational Administration*, *41*(2), 171–

185.

https://doi.org/10.1108/09578230310464675

Searby, L., Ballenger, J., & Tripses, J. (2015).

Climbing the ladder, holding the ladder: The

mentoring experience of higher education

female leaders. *Educational Management Administration & Leadership*, *42*(6), 808–824. https://doi.org/10.21423/awlj-v35.a141

Sedivy-Benton, A., Strohschen, G., Cavazos, N., & Boden-McGill, C. (2014). Good ol' boys, mean girls, and tyrants: A phenomenological study of the lived experiences and survival strategies of bullied women adult educators. *Adult Learning*, *26*(1), 35–41. https://doi.org/10.1177/1045159514558411

Seidman, I. (2013). *Interviewing as qualitative research: A guide for researchers in education and the social sciences.* Teachers College Press.

Sergiovanni, T. J. (2001). *The principalship: A reflective practice perspective.* Allyn and Bacon.

Showers, J. (1985, April). Teachers coaching teachers. *Educational Leadership, 42,* 43–48.

Sincar, M. (2013). Challenges school principals facing in the context of technology leadership. *Education Sciences: Theory & Practice, 13*(2), 1273–1284. https://files.eric.ed.gov/fulltext/EJ1017245.pdf

Sipe, C. L. (1996). *Mentoring: A synthesis of P/PV's research: 1988–1995.* Public/Private Ventures.

Smalley, S., Hawkins, J., & Lukman R. (2021). Students' initial response to the Covid-19 remote learning transition: A pilot study. *The Internet Journal of Allied Health Sciences and Practice, 19*(3).

Smith, W., & Benavot, A. (2019). Improving accountability in education: The importance of structured democratic voice. *Asia Pacific Education Review, 20*(2), 193–205. https://doi.org/10.1007/s12564-019-09599-9

Smith, J. A., & Shinebourne, P. (2012). Interpretative phenomenological analysis. In H. Cooper, P. M. Camic, D. L. Long, A. T. Panter, D. Rindskopf, & K. J. Sher (Eds.), *APA handbook of research methods in psychology* (Vol. 2. Research designs:

Quantitative, qualitative,

neuropsychological, and biological, pp. 73–

82). American Psychological Association.

https://doi.org/10.1037/13620-005

Sol, K. (2021) Distributed leadership in schools: A

brief review of the literature. *Cambodian*

Journal Educational Research, 1(1), 73–80.

Spillane, J. P. (2006). *Distributed leadership.*

Jossey-Bass.

Stein, M. K., & D'Amico, L. (2000). *How subjects*

matter in school leadership. Paper presented

at the annual meeting of the American

Educational Research Association, New

Orleans, LA.

Stein, M. K., & Nelson, B. S. (2003). Leadership content knowledge. *Educational Evaluation and Policy Analysis*, *25*(4), 423–448.

Sterrett, W. (2013). *Short on time: How do I make time to lead and learn as a principal?* ASCD.

Sterrett, W. (2016). *Igniting teacher leadership: How do I empower my teachers to lead and learn?* ASCD.

Strack, R., Kugel, J., Dyrchs, S., & Tauber, M. (2020). *Leadership in the new now.* Boston Consulting Group.

Studies in Continuing Education. (2015). Professionalism and practice: Critical understandings of professional learning and education. *Studies in Continuing Education,*

171

37(2), 125–130.

http://dx.doi.org/10.1080/0158037X.2015.1032921

Sun, A. (2018). Grow your own leaders: On-the-job mentoring for aspiring assistant principals. *Journal of Behavior and Social Sciences*, *5*, 107–117.

Taggart, G. L., & Wilson, A. P. (2005). *Promoting reflective thinking in teachers* (2nd ed.). Corwin Press.

Tehrani, N. (2004). Bullying: A source of chronic posttraumatic stress? *British Journal of Guidance & Counseling*, *32*(3).

The Wallace Foundation. (2012, June). *The making of the principal: Five lessons in leadership training.* Author.

Thomas, L. G., & Knezek, D. (1991). Providing technology leadership for restructured schools. *Journal of Research on Computing in Education, 24*(2), 265–279. https://doi.org/10.1080/08886504.1991.1078 2008

VanTuyle, V. L. (2018). Illinois assistant principals: Instructional leaders or disciplinarians. *Education Leadership Review, 19*(1), 1–20. Retrieved from https://files.eric.ed.gov/fulltext/EJ1200805.p df

Vick, L. C. (2011). *Assistant principals' perceptions: Knowledge, skills, and attributes for effective leadership.* Faculty of the College of Education University of Houston.

Varalakshmi, R., & Arunachalam, K. (2020). COVID 2019 – role of faculty members to keep mental activeness of students. *Asian Journal of Psychiatry*, *51*, 102091. https://doi.org/10.1016/j.ajp.2020.102091

Walsh, E., & Dotter, D. (2018). The impact of replacing principals on student achievement in District of Columbia public schools. *Education Finance and Policy*, *15*(3), 518–542.

Wanberg, C. R., Hooft, E.A., Liu, S., Csillag, B. (2019). *Can job seekers achieve more through networking? The role networking intensity, self-efficacy, and proximal*

benefits: Personnel Psychology. Wiley.

Wang, C. (2010). Technology leadership among

school principals: A technology-

coordinator's perspective. *Asian Social*

Science, 6(1), 51–54.

Wang, G., Zhang, Y., Zhao, J., Zhang, J., & Jiang,

F. (2020). Mitigate the effects of home

confinement on children during the COVID-

19 outbreak. *Lancet, 395,* 945–947.

https://doi.org/10.1016/S0140-

6736(20)30547-X

Wasden, D. (1988). *Organizational entry:*

Recruitment, selection, and socialization of

Newcomers. Addison-Wesley.

Wassenaar, C. L., & Pearce, C. L. (2012). The nature of shared leadership. In J. Antonakis & D. Day (Eds.), *The nature of leadership* (pp. 363–389). Prentice Hall.

Weiner, E. J. (2003). Secretary Paulo Freire and the democratization of power: Toward a theory of transformative leadership. *Educational Philosophy and Theory*, *35*(1), 89–106.

Weller, L. D., & Weller, S. J. (2002). *The assistant principal: Essentials for effective school leadership.* Corwin Press.

Yammarino, F. J., & Bass, B. M. (1990). Transformational leadership and multiple levels of analysis. *Human Relations*, *43*, 975–995.

https://doi.org/10.1177/00187267900430100
3

Yoon, S. Y. (2016). Exploring learner perspectives on learner autonomy for blended learning in EFL conversation classes. *STEM Journal*, *17*(1), 197–220.

Yu, Z., Xu, W., & Yu, L. (2022). Constructing an online sustainable educational model in COVID-19 pandemic environments. *Sustainability*, *14*(6), 3598. https://doi.org/10.3390/su14063598

Zapf, D., Knoz, C., & Kulla, M. (1996). On the relationship between mobbing factors and job content, social work environment and health outcomes. *European Journal of Work and Organisational Psychology*, *5*(2), 215–237.

Zhu, X., & Liu, J. (2020, April). Education in and after covid-19: Immediate responses and long-term visions. *Postdigital Science and Education*. https://doi.org/10.1007/s42438-020-00126-3

APPENDIX A
INFORMED CONSENT FORM

<u>CONSENT FORM</u>

PUBLIC SCHOOL ADMINISTRATOR'S PERCEPTIONS ON BEST LEADERSHIP PRACTICES AND
PROFESSIONAL DEVELOPMENT STRATEGIES FOR CAREER ADVANCEMENT OF ASSISTANT PRINCIPALS

You are invited to participate in a study of public-school administrators' perceptions on best leadership practices and professional development strategies for the career advancement of assistant principals.

My name is Tiffany Burks, and I am a doctoral student at Fayetteville State University, in the office Educational Leadership. I hope to gain a better understanding about public-school administrator's perceptions on best leadership practices and professional development. You will be one of 20 participants chosen to participate in this study.

If you decide to participate, you may be asked in the following phases of data collection (A) Answer and return demographic questions via email. (B) Participate in a Zoom interview that will be audio and virtual recorded.. (C) Respond to my follow-up email for interpretation accuracy. You may decide not to participate in any task or you may decide to not answer any questions on the questionnaire, inventories, or during the interviews that make you feel uncomfortable or embarrassed; you may stop participation at any time during the study. There is no monetary compensation for participation in this study. I will make all reasonable efforts to accommodate your schedule and time constraints.

Any information that is obtained in connection with this study and that can be identified with you will remain confidential and will be disclosed only with your permission. Audio tapes and transcription, journal field notes will be kept under lock and key. All audio tapes will be erased following data collection, analysis, and manuscript development. At no time will your name or institution be identified in reports, papers, or publications.

Your decision whether or not to participate will not affect your future relations with Fayetteville State University. If you decide to participate, you are free to discontinue participation at any time.

You are making a decision whether or not to participate. Your signature indicates that you have read the information provided above and that you have decided to participate. You may withdraw at any time after signing this form, should you choose to discontinue your participation in this study.

If you have questions, please ask me. If you have additional questions later, I will be happy to answer them. You can reach me at 910-489-4528 or tmcmil17@broncos.uncfsu.edu or write me at Tiffany Burks, 3139 Wisteria Lane #201, Fayetteville, NC 28314 You can also contact my dissertation chair, Dr. Linda Wilson-Jones at lwilson-jones@uncfsu.edu or at 910-672-1634. If you have questions or concerns, at any time during this study, about your rights as a research subject you may contact:

Dr. Theodore Kaniuka, Chair of the Human Rights in Research Committee
Fayetteville State University
Fayetteville, NC 28301-4298
(910) 672-1636

You may keep a blank copy of this form for your records.

_____   _____
Signature of Participant   Date   Signature of Investigator   Date

This project has been approved by the Fayetteville State University Institutional Review Board Human Rights in Research Committee (Phone: 910-672-1569)

APPENDIX B
IRB APPROVAL

FAYETTEVILLE
STATE UNIVERSITY

April 29, 2021

TO:	Tiffany Burks
IRB#:	2021-P-0035
Study:	Public School Administrator's Perceptions on Best Leadership Practices and Professional Development Strategies For Career Advancement of Assistant Principals
RE:	Approval
Submission:	New
Co-PIs:	None
Expiration:	April 28, 2022

Upon review, your human subject research application, assigned IRB # 2021-P-0035, has been **Approved under Exempt Status** by the Human Rights in Research Committee (HRRC). This study was reviewed in accordance with federal regulations governing human subjects research including those found at 45 CFR 46 (Common Rule), 45 CFR 164 (HIPAA), where applicable.

Please be reminded that you are *required* to indicate your study number on all documents relating to your study. If you have any questions, please feel free to contact Dr. Theodore Kaniuka, Chair of the HRRC, tkaniuka@uncfsu.edu. Please reference your proposal title and number in all electronic communications.

This study was reviewed in accordance with federal regulations governing human subjects research including those found at 45 CFR 46 (Common Rule), 45 CFR 164 (HIPAA), where applicable.

Sincerely,

Dr. Theodore Kaniuka
Chair- Human Rights in Research Committee

Office of Sponsored Research and Programs
1200 Murchison Road / Fayetteville, North Carolina 28801-4298 / 910-672-1569 / 910-672-2110 / www.uncfsu.edu/research